Weighing up the Evidence

TIMELINE:

The Welfare State

Michael Rawcliffe

Dryad Press, London

Contents

Typeset by Tek-Art Ltd, Kent
and printed in Great Britain by
The Bath Press, Bath
for the Publishers
Dryad Press,
4 Fitzhardinge Street,
London W1H 0AH

ISBN 0 85219 806 X

ACKNOWLEDGMENTS

The illustrations on pages 45, 49, 52 and 55 are courtesy
B.T. Batsford Ltd; all other illustrations are courtesy
Michael Rawcliffe. Front cover illustrations: (*left*): a
modern hospital operating theatre (*courtesy NHS*); (*top
right*): Aneurin Bevan; (*bottom right*): *Punch* comments
on the 1908 Children's Act.

Introduction

This book is concerned with the developments which led to the emergence of the Welfare State. The Welfare State can mean a variety of things: in this book it is defined as the provision by the State of the basic essentials of life, if the individual or family is unable to cope. In other words, the State has come to believe that it should be concerned, and help those who, without assistance, would suffer. In our time the Social Services which carry out this function are concerned with such groups as the old, the sick and the disabled. The Welfare State was not fully introduced in Britain until after the Second World War, in 1948.

Before the State came to take an active part, the individual who fell sick, was injured, or was too young or too old to work was dependent upon his or her family, or failing that, charity. In medieval times charity was largely the concern of the Church. Sometimes the employer might help, but there was no legal obligation to do so.

By the sixteenth century the population had grown considerably and Parliament decided that the Parish should be responsible for the paupers within its boundaries, and so the Church was given an important secular role. Each Parish was allowed to raise a poor rate to provide support for those in need and by the eighteenth century a wide variety of Poor Law schemes were in operation.

The late eighteenth century saw revolutions in both agriculture and industry in Britain. Many people were attracted to work in the factories in the expanding towns as a more commercial agriculture led to a surplus of population on the land. Not only was there a movement of population, but also a rapid rise in population, especially in the growing towns and cities. Whilst the standard of living probably rose, urban conditions were poor, and the towns were unable to accommodate the rapid population growth. Slums developed, diseases spread and unemployment was sometimes high. By the end of the Napoleonic Wars in 1815, many people felt that an unfair burden was being placed on the ratepayer as the Poor Rates increased. The ideas developed that the poor were perhaps not being helped by being supported and that indiscriminate aid was leading to a growing number of paupers, who had lost the will to work. There were also calls for greater efficiency in the spending of the money.

The result was the Poor Law Amendment Act of 1834 which only gave relief (help) to the able bodied inside the workhouse. Inside the workhouse living conditions were to be so severe that the poor would only seek help as a matter of last resort. It was hoped that this would result in a decrease in those seeking Poor Relief and a decrease in the amount being spent.

This system lasted until 1929, with many features remaining until 1948. The amount of money spent did fall, but private charity was still necessary. By the 1870s it was realized that self-help was a worthy aim for those who could help themselves, but that a significant number did not fall into this category, and needed help from another source.

During the nineteenth century various surveys revealed the problem to the comfortably off and richer groups in society. Various charitable organizations developed and the Churches became actively involved. Also Christians outside the Church, such as William Booth and Dr Barnardo, did much to help, whilst pressure for reform was exerted within Parliament by MPs such as the Earl of Shaftesbury, and outside Parliament by various pressure groups. By the end of the century both political parties had come to accept that certain groups within society needed the protection of the law.

By the early twentieth century the State had appointed inspectors for schools, factories and mines. Public health and housing legislation had given local authorities permission to raise rates, appoint Medical Officers of Health, introduce bye-laws and clear slums. Cities such as Birmingham had made considerable progress under reforming mayors.

However, various enquiries into the conditions of the poor had shown that all was not well. Britain by 1900 was undoubtedly rich, but the gulf between the rich and the poor remained. In fact redevelopment in the cities for new shopping centres, railway stations, or simply for broader streets had led to the spread of the slums because there were not enough houses or rooms available at a low rent. There was still a wide gulf between the life chances of those living in the suburbs and those in the worst inner city areas.

The feeling developed that in order to remain a Great Power Britain must increase the health and standards of *all* her people. Nations such as Germany and the USA were overtaking us industrially, and Germany had already introduced state insurance and pension schemes in the 1880s.

Thus the period 1906-1914, with the Liberal Party in power, saw the first real series of social reforms. Old age pensions and insurance (health and unemployment) were amongst the reforms which showed that the State had accepted its responsibility to care for the sick, old, young and needy. They were to be helped by old age pensions, national insurance and a Children's Act.

Between the two world wars there were many problems, notably of housing and unemployment, placing great strains on government and local resources. By the 1930s words such as slump, depression, dole and means test were well-known and the economic health of the country did not improve until the Second World War.

During the Second World War Britain was governed by a coalition which introduced an Education Act in 1944 and commissioned an inquiry into the social services, with Lord Beveridge as its Chairman. A report was published in 1942. The first postwar election in 1945 resulted in the return of the Labour Party, which introduced the National Health Service Act of 1946, which is regarded as the beginning of the Welfare State.

Forty years on the debate on the Welfare State has begun anew. All parties acknowledge that the State must maintain a basic responsibility for those in need, but are divided over the degree of help which should be given, and how far people should become more independent. The present Conservative Government led by Mrs Thatcher would like individuals to take more responsibility for their present and future needs, rather than assuming that the State will care for them in every way. Equally, charities are urged to play a greater role, whilst private health schemes are being encouraged to provide alternatives or supplement the existing National Health system.

This book is about the development of the Welfare State, and the growing responsibility of the State for the individual. It is also about money; the amount which the State should contribute out of taxation and national insurance and the money which the individual should spend on his or her own health, contribute to private health insurance schemes or give to charity.

You will find that many of the arguments in the current debate have a familiar ring. Cost, charity, the role of the individual and the family, and the role of the State are constant themes throughout much of this book. This demonstrates the continuity of history. You will also find that circumstances differ and that intervening events play a part. This is the other vital historical element of change. The understanding of the ideas of continuity and change in history will help you to come to some understanding of how the present has been arrived at, and how we may proceed in the future.

You will also find that at all periods in the past, and also in the present, a variety of views are presented, which may derive from factors such as age, sex, wealth, class and even where one lives. This may seem obvious, but all too often people look back to the past and see, for example, the Victorians as all thinking in the same way. Make sure you look up unfamiliar words so that you understand the meaning of the contemporary writers. After reading this book you will come to understand that the Victorians and peoples of any period had differing sets of values and ideas, beyond the minimum agreement necessary for an ordered society.

The Nineteenth Century 1800–1870

The money spent by a Suffolk overseer of the poor, 1800. What was the major expense?

History does not just show us the steady progression from the past to the present. The period discussed in this chapter shows this quite clearly; our approach is to look at the problems which the people faced at this time. These were centred around the rapid growth of industry (industrialization), the rapid rise in the size of towns and cities (urbanization) and the overall growth of population, especially in the former.

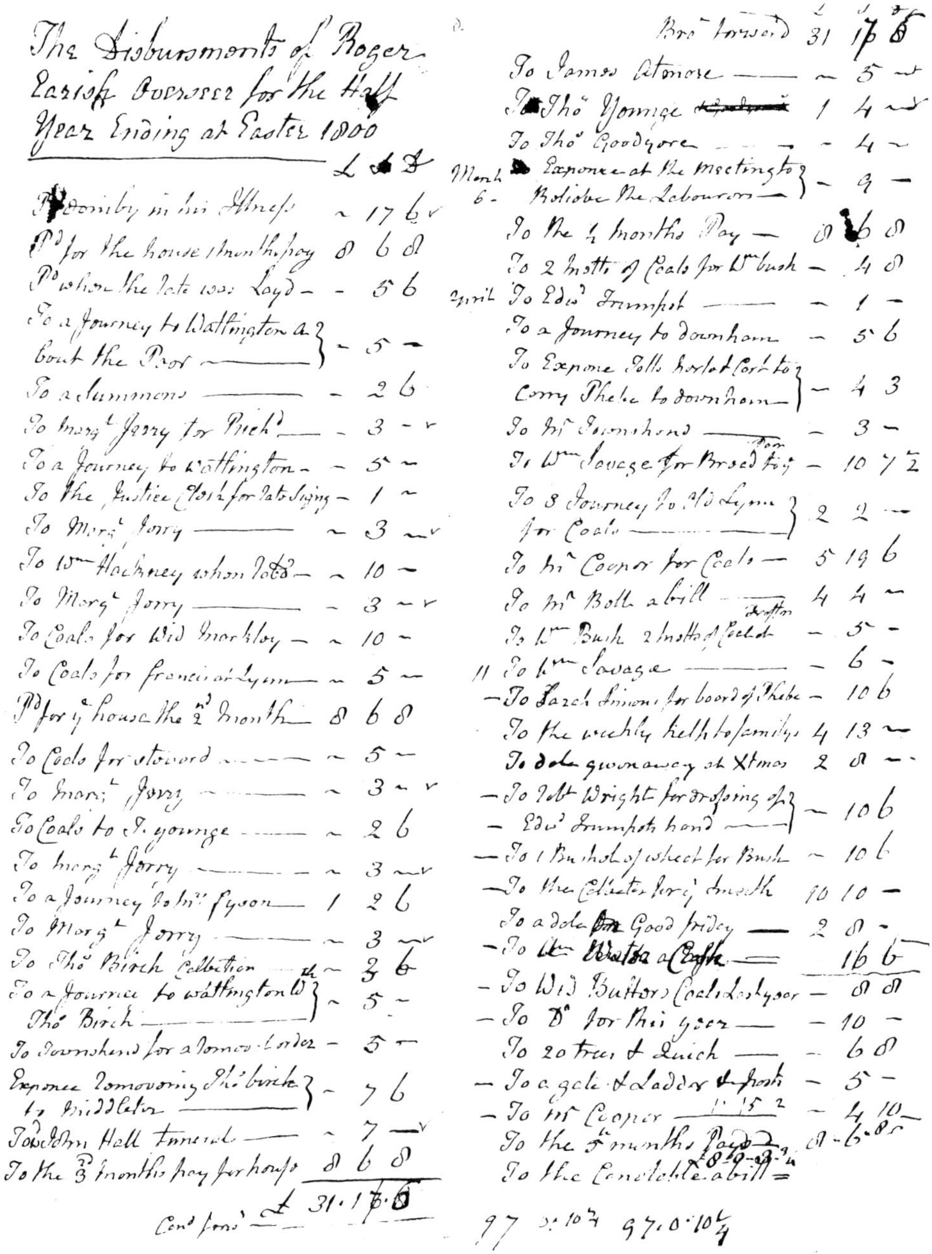

The Disbursments of Roger Parish Overseer for the Half Year Ending at Easter 1800

	£	s	d
Pd Domby in his Illness	–	17	6
Pd for the house 1 months pay	8	6	8
Pd when the rate was Layd	–	5	6
To a Journey to Wattington about the Poor	–	5	–
To a Summons	–	2	6
To Marg^t Jerry for Pick^d	–	3	–
To a Journey to Wattington	–	5	–
To the Justice Clerk for Rate Signing	–	1	–
To Marg^t Jerry	–	3	–
To Wm Hackney when Poor^d	–	10	–
To Marg^t Jerry	–	3	–
To Coals for Wid Markley	–	10	–
To Coals for Francis at Lynn	–	5	–
Pd for ye house the 2^d Month	8	6	8
To Coals for Steward	–	5	–
To Marg^t Jerry	–	3	–
To Coals to T. Younge	–	2	6
To Marg^t Jerry	–	3	–
To a Journey to Mr Fyson	1	2	6
To Marg^t Jerry	–	3	–
To Thos Birch Collection	–	2	6
To a Journey to Wattington W^th Thos Birch	–	5	–
To Townshend for a Remove Order	–	5	–
Expence Removing Thos Birch to Middleton	–	7	6
To Wm Hall Funeral	–	7	–
To the 3^d months pay for house	8	6	8
	£ 31	17	6

Cont forw^d

	£	s	d
Bro^t forward	31	17	6
To James Atmore	–	5	–
To Thos Younge	1	4	–
To Thos Goodyore	–	4	–
March 6 – Expence at the meeting to Relieve the Labourers	–	9	–
To the 4 Months Pay	8	6	8
To 2 Chaldron of Coals for Wm Bush	–	4	8
April To Edwd Trumpet	–	1	–
To a Journey to Downham	–	5	6
To Expence Tolls horse & Cart to Carry Phebe to Downham	–	4	3
To Mr Townshend	–	3	–
To Wm Savage for Bread for Poor	–	10	7½
To 8 Journey to Old Lynn for Coals	2	2	–
To Mr Cooper for Coals	5	19	6
To Mr Bell a bill	4	4	–
To Wm Bush 2 Chaldron of Coals	–	5	–
11 To Wm Savage	–	6	–
To Sarah Simons for board of Phebe	–	10	6
To the weekly Relief to familys	4	13	–
To dole given away at Xtmas	2	8	–
To Robt Wright for dressing of Edwd Trumpets hand	–	10	6
To 1 Bushel of wheat for Bush	–	10	6
To the Collector [illegible]	10	10	–
To a dole on Good Friday	2	8	–
To Wm Watts a Coffin	–	16	6
To Wid Butters Coals Last year	–	8	8
To D^o for this year	–	10	–
To 20 trees & Quick	–	6	8
To a gate & Ladder & posts	–	5	–
To Mr Cooper	–	4	10
To the 5 months Pay	8	6	8
To the Constable a bill			

97 0 10¾   97.0.10¼

The population of cities in Britain 1801-61
(in thousands)

	1801	1811	1821	1831	1841	1851	1861
Birmingham	71	83	102	144	183	233	296
Glasgow	77	101	147	202	275	345	420
Leeds	53	63	84	123	152	172	207
Liverpool	82	104	138	202	286	376	444
Manchester	75	89	126	182	235	303	339

(*Source:* Census Population Tables, 1801-61)

Which decade saw the greatest overall growth in population and which city saw the greatest overall increase?

The Industrial Revolution had been begun by numerous individuals taking risks, investing, and introducing new processes and methods of working. By the 1820s a factory system had developed and such cities as Manchester seemed to be the cities of the future with their high-rise factories working 24 hours a day, with the labour force living close by in tightly-packed terraces, or in back-to-back houses, where little light or air could penetrate. The new labour force had come to the cities of their own free will, prepared to work long hours, and earned more than in the countryside. However, the disadvantages were great — long hours worked by all including children; industrial polution in the atmosphere through coal-burning factory chimneys, and in the rivers through human excrement and industrial waste. Add to this the further public health problems caused by the density of population and the sub-standard housing, the lack of an adequate means of either sewage disposal, pure water or unadulterated food.

Average age of death

	Gentlemen, professional persons and their families	Tradesmen and their families	Labourers and artisans and their families
Manchester	38	20	17
Bolton	34	23	18
Bethnal Green	45	26	16
Liverpool	35	22	15
Leeds	44	27	19
Kendal (Cumbria)	45	39	34
Rutland (county)	52	41	38

(*Source:* Adapted from Chadwick; *Sanitary Conditions in England and Wales*, 1842)

What conclusions can you draw from these figures?

Finally, there was the problem of occasional unemployment, for with the industrial slumps a workforce might be laid off; this was particularly severe in a small town dependent on a single industry, such as cotton.

In 1848 an anonymous pamphleteer wrote:

> The great duties of social life must be thoroughly taught and expounded, not to a few, but to all, without exception, the habits and dispositions being trained in conformity. These duties are: to strive to the utmost to be self-supporting – not to be a burden upon any other man or upon society . . . to make such use of all superior advantages whether of knowledge, skill or wealth, as to promote, on all occasions, the general happiness of mankind.
>
> (*Source:* Anon, *A Few Questions on Secular Education* (1842), quoted in D. Fraser, *The Evolution of the Welfare State*, Macmillan, 1978)

This is the philosophy of self help held by many at that time. Improvement would come only from one's own effort. What might have been the contemporary counter-argument?

THE MOVEMENT FOR FACTORY REFORM

Children had been working long hours in factories for 50 years before the 1833 Factory Act, but in the latter years pressure groups had developed outside Parliament which were determined to improve the lot of those who could not help themselves.

The classical argument against government intervention was expressed by Macaulay to the electors in the Leeds election in 1832.

> The best government cannot act directly and suddenly and violently on the comforts of the people; it cannot rain down provisions into their houses; it cannot give them bread, meat and wine; these things they can only obtain by their own honest industry and to protect them in that honest industry and secure to them its fruits is the end of all honest government . . . . The general rule – a rule not more beneficial to the capitalist than to the labourer – is that contracts shall be free and that the state shall not interfere between the master and the workman. To this general rule there is an exception. Children cannot protect themselves and are therefore entitled to the protection of the public.
>
> (*Source: Leeds Mercury*, 16 June 1832)

In the following year a Government Commission reported that:

> . . . at the age when children suffer these injuries from the labour they undergo, they are not free agents, but are let out to hire, the wages they earn being received and appropriated by their parents and guardians.
>
> We are therefore of opinion that a case is made out for the interference of the Legislature on behalf of the children employed in factories.
>
> (*Source: First Report of the Factory Commissioners*, 1833)

What is the major point in common between these two very different primary sources? Do you think that Macaulay's argument might have lost him votes amongst the factory owners?

The result of the recommendations was the Factory Act of 1833, which limited the hours which 9 to 13 year olds could work to eight hours a day and appointed four inspectors to enforce the Act. The Act was to be applied to all textile mills, except silk and lace.

The next breach in laissez-faire came in the mining industry where both children and women worked underground in appalling conditions. Lord Ashley pressed for a commission of enquiry whose illustrated report shocked the nation. The result was the Mines Act of 1842. Harriet Martineau, a believer in laissez-faire, reluctantly felt that the Act was necessary.

The great majority of the nation, however, felt that it was better to have a large burden thrown on the parishes for a time than to let such abuses continue; that, making every allowance for exaggeration, the facts were horrible; and that, the labour-market being already interfered with by Factory Bills, this was not the point to stop at. So the bill passed, with some amendments which Lord Ashley submitted to, rather than wait. By this bill, women were excluded from mining and colliery labour altogether.

(*Source:* H. Martineau, *History of the Peace*, Chambers, 1858)

How had the 1833 and 1842 Acts interfered with the labour market?

By 1880 the principle of state intervention on behalf of women and children had been established, as had the principle of inspection.

THE POOR LAW

In 1834 the Poor Law Commissioners reported. They put forward strong arguments why the existing system of poor relief, based upon the Parish, should be reformed. Many of their ideas were accepted, and in the Poor Law Amendment Act of 1834 Parishes were to be grouped into Poor Law Unions and a locally elected Board of Guardians was to be in control. The major recommendation that was incorporated into the Act was that the able-bodied should only receive relief inside the workhouse and that the conditions there should be such as to deter them from applying. The Commissioners had found that where strictness had been applied, pauperism had been reduced.

We have seen that in every instance in which the able-bodied labourers have been rendered independent of partial relief, or of relief otherwise than in a well-regulated workhouse –

1. Their industry has been restored and improved.

2. Frugal habits have been created or strengthened.

3. The permanent demand for their labour has increased.

4. And the increase has been such, that their wages, so far from being depressed by the increased amount of labour on the market, have in general advanced.

5. The number of improvident and wretched marriages has diminished.

6. Their discontent has been abated, and their moral and social condition in every way improved . . . .

(*Source: Report of the Poor Law Commissioners*, 1834)

What benefits do the Commissioners envisage if their recommendations are implemented?

In 1835 and 1836 Poor Law Unions were formed in the south of England. The Dulwich Board of Guardians was formed in November 1835. The board of guardians was established under the provisions of the Poor Law Act on 24 November 1835, and the following particulars are taken from the first annual report of the board (1836): on 31 December 1835, the total number of indoor poor was 267, divided as follows: men, 75; women, 126; children, 66. In the same year the recipients of outdoor relief numbered 1,700 – 242 men, 538 women, and 920 children. Within 12 months of the new act coming into operation, a marked change had been brought about, as, on 31 December 1836, the number of outdoor poor had been reduced from 1,700 to 605; whilst the total indoor poor had increased from 267 to 271.

It may be considered by many individuals, that reduction in the allowance to the poor cannot by possibility have bettered their condition, but only have deprived them of a few comforts previously enjoyed, and that the loss is far more deeply and severely felt by them than the proportionate saving is appreciated by the ratepayer; but such, the board are convinced from experience, is not the case. So far from the individuals whose relief has been discontinued being sufferers by the change, the board have in their possession a list of no less than 207 persons, the greater portion of whom are still resident within the parish, the numerical number of whose families amounts to 664, who under the old system were regular in their attendance at the board of parochial relief, but are now maintaining themselves and their families solely by their own industry and labour; while the difference between what they were and what they are, both as to morals and comfort, is most remarkable.

In the former case, while they leaned on parochial aid, most of them bore idle and dissolute characters, their families were ragged and starved, and their hovels filthy and wretched. In the latter case, now that they depend on their own energies, they readily find employment – are reported industrious; whilst their children are decently clad and go to school, and their dwellings present the appearance which would be desired in the cottage of an English labourer.

(*Source: Annual Report of the Dulwich Board of Guardians*, 1836)

Does the case of Dulwich prove that the 1834 Act was successful? How should this evidence be judged?

However even in the south of England the introduction of the new Poor Law was not always achieved peacefully. In the First Annual Report of the

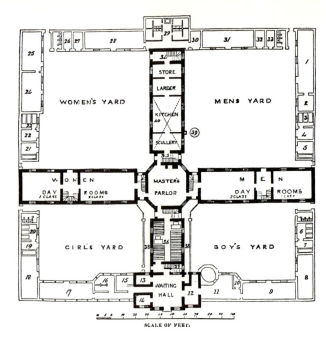

1 Work Room.	22 Bath.
2 Store.	23 Receiving Ward, 3 beds.
3 Receiving Wards, 3 beds.	24 Laundry.
4 Bath.	25 Wash-house.
5 Washing Room.	26 Dead House.
6 Receiving Ward, 3 beds.	27 Refractory Ward.
7 Washing Room.	28 Work Room.
8 Work Room.	29 Piggery.
9 Flour and Mill Room.	30 Slaughter House.
10 Coals.	31 Work Room.
11 Bakehouse.	32 Refractory Ward.
12 Bread Room.	33 Dead House.
13 Searching Room.	34 Women's Stairs to Dining Hall.
14 Porter's Room.	35 Men's Stairs to ditto.
15 Store.	36 Boys' and Girls' School and Dining Room.
16 Potatoes.	37 Delivery.
17 Coals.	38 Passage.
18 Work Room	39 Well.
19 Washing Room.	40 Cellar under ground.
20 Receiving Ward, 3 beds.	
21 Washing Room.	

Plan for a workhouse, from the 1st Annual Report of the Poor Law Commissioners, 1835. Note the way in which the family is divided.

Poor Law Commissioners published in 1835 the Commissioners comment on the reaction to the abolition of the allowance system and the creation of the Board of Guardians:

In East Kent the riots were promptly suppressed by the civil authorities, with the aid of two serjeants of police, and the presence of a party of military. Some disturbances were threatened at Eastbourne, but were prevented by the energy and vigilance of the magistrates. A riot occurred in the Ampthill union, but was quelled by the active aid of a party of 20 of the Metropolitan Police, the yeomanry being ready to act, if required. One riot which occurred at Chesham, Bucks, was suppressed by the energy of the local authorities, who were afterwards aided in apprehending some of the ringleaders, and in maintaining the peace, by a body of the same number of the Metropolitan Police and a party of yeomanry. In a few other instances the relieving officers have been assaulted in the execution of their duty.

(*Source: First Annual Report of the Poor Law Commissioners, 1835*)

The Commissioners' official explanation was that the riots were largely caused by the rule that if outdoor relief was given, half of it must be in bread. The quality was not in dispute, but they observed that the agitators were the shopkeepers who felt that they would lose trade.

What different sorts of arguments might have been used by a farm labourer who actually participated in the disturbances? How would he have reacted to the intervention of the Metropolitan Police?

In 1837 the system was applied to the north of England and here it was met with a much stronger reaction because it coincided with an industrial depression and many able bodied workers were unemployed through no fault of their own. They were not idle, but many happened to be living in cotton towns where there was no other work. An Anti-Poor Law Movement grew up which resisted the introduction of the Poor Law Union and called the new workhouses, "Bastilles". In addition, in some areas ratepayers were elected Guardians in order to *oppose* the building of a new union workhouse.

When there was distress and pressure of numbers upon the workhouse accommodation, the guardians rejected the building of a new workhouse because of heavy rates, and when times were good and there were few workhouse inmates the guardians rejected a new workhouse as unnecessary.

(*Source:* R. Boyson, quoted in M.A. Crowther, *The Workhouse System*, Methuen, 1983)

Fortunately the New Poor Law was not so rigidly applied as historians once believed, and by 1854 84% of paupers were on outdoor relief, outside the workhouse. Nevertheless, as Lloyd George was to realize at the beginning of the twentieth century, whilst the Poor Law provided a last resort,

Conditions under which this system had hitherto worked have been so harsh and humiliating that working class pride revolts against accepting so degrading and doubtful a boon.

(*Source:* H.N. Bunbury (ed.), *Lloyd George's Ambulance Wagon*, 1957)

Try and find out what conditions Lloyd George had in mind.

PUBLIC HEALTH   In 1842 the Report on the *Sanitary Conditions of the Labouring Population of England and Wales* was published. The writing was almost entirely the work of Edwin Chadwick. He had played a large part in the report on the Poor Law and again his utilitarian views are evident. He was no respecter of tradition and believed in efficiency and the abolition of waste. He was appalled at the great loss of life each year through preventable disease:

In general all epidemics and all infectious diseases are attended with charges, immediate and ultimate, on the Poor Rates. Labourers are suddenly thrown by infectious disease into a state of destitution, for which immediate relief must be given. In the case of death the widow and the children are thrown as paupers on the parish. The amount of burthens thus produced is frequently so great as to render it good economy on the part of the administrators of the Poor Laws to incur the charges for preventing the evils where they are ascribable to physical causes . . . .

(*Source:* Quoted by S.E. Finer, *Life and Times of Edwin Chadwick*, 1957)

Which influential groups in the local community would be persuaded by this argument?

Chadwick was also concerned with the dangers to society resulting from the early death of the head of the family and the lack of family stability. In one section of the Report he wrote that:

> In the metropolis the experience is similar. The mobs against which the police have to guard come from the most depressed districts; and the constant report of the superintendents is, that scarcely any old men are to be seen amongst them. In general they appear to consist of persons between 16 and 25 years of age. The mobs from such districts as Bethnal Green are proportionately conspicuous for a deficiency of bodily strength, without, however, being from that cause proportionately the less dangerously mischievous. I was informed by peace officers that the great havoc at Bristol was committed by mere boys.

Would this appeal to the same groups as the previous argument or would it have a broader appeal? How has Chadwick extended his argument?

The 1842 Report did not immediately lead to parliamentary legislation, but certainly influenced public opinion. Perhaps of as much influence were the various cholera outbreaks which affected everyone. Gradually during the next 30 years the government began to introduce laws which allowed local authorities to take action and introduce bye-laws against such people as builders where their housing was sub-standard, to clear slums and appoint Officers of Health. Cities such as Birmingham were often in the forefront of reform with slum clearance schemes, inner city development and the taking over of the small privately run water and gas companies.

We can see at the local level the breaching of laissez-faire as the town and city councils began to take on responsibility which many had earlier felt was an infringement of individual liberties. Nevertheless cost remained an important issue and many wealthier ratepayers resented higher rates from which they could not see a direct benefit. In addition the local councils were often resentful of what they regarded as state interference.

CARING FOR THE SICK

Only the rich could afford medical bills and those outside the Poor Law system had to rely on hospitals supported by voluntary subscriptions, and the general dispensaries of these hospitals which often provided the medicines. In addition medical clubs and friendly societies were encouraged to try and promote self-help and independence amongst the working groups.

By 1850 some 72 per cent of all paupers were seeking relief due to sickness. Thus it was that with the Poor Law a basic health service was developed. But in 1841 another fear had been raised, that it might be too efficient:

> If the pauper is always promptly attended by a skilful and well-qualified medical practitioner – if the patient be furnished with all the cordials and stimulants which may promote his recovery . . . [it will] encourage a resort to the poor rates for medical relief.

(*Source:* Seventh Annual Report of the Poor Law Commissioners)

How far do you believe that this fear is a justifiable one?

A printed envelope advertising the temperance movement, c 1850. Note the contrasts between the left and right sides of the envelope.

In 1853 vaccination became compulsory for all infants, and it was to be given to those who could not afford the fees, by the Poor Law Unions. In time it became available free to all those who were outside the Poor Law, but could not afford the private doctor's fee. Additionally the Poor Law hospitals came to take in the sick from within the Union who were not paupers.

Thus the Poor Law came to provide a real service to the local community. As a leading economist, Thorold Rogers, said in 1870:

A poor rate is an insurance of the labourer's life and health. It maintains him in old age, assists him in sickness and protects him when labouring under mental disease, and supplies him with the services of a highly skilled person in the shape of a medical officer . . . . At the existing rate of agricultural wages a farm labourer and to some extent the artisan could hardly supply these services for himself.

(*Source:* Quoted by R.G. Hodgkinson, *The origins of the National Health Service*, The Wellcome Institute, 1967)

In time the Poor Law Union hospitals came to be separated from the Union Workhouse and the local community often regarded them as "state" hospitals.

ON REFLECTION:

The new Poor Law brought increased efficiency and savings to the ratepayer, at the expense of a tighter and harsher regime for the pauper. Do you think that the modern welfare state emerged out of the changes that came about during the 1840s? Would Lloyd George's later comments (see page 11) on the shortcomings of the Poor Law have been understood in 1850?

The Late Victorian Period: 1870–1900

CHANGING ATTITUDES TOWARDS THE POOR

Samuel Smiles in his famous book *Self Help* (1851) believed that the growing wealth of Britain which had become "the workshop of the world" by 1851, would enable every individual who wished to escape from poverty to do so by hard work. The Great Exhibition held in that year attracted huge crowds to London to see the achievements of British industry and commerce. It was a time of great optimism and hope. But by the 1870s the mid-Victorian view of self-help was coming to be seen as inadequate.

In 1881 Henry George's book *Progress and Poverty* was published. The title deliberately emphasized the relationship between the two as by this time many had realized that, whilst Britain had progressed and the national wealth had risen, the poor still remained. In many ways the consequences of prosperity in the great cities – rising land values and house prices – made the housing of the poor an increasingly difficult problem. The very success of industry, reflected by a city skyline of factories, warehouses and chimneys belching out smoke and polluting rivers, made health a particular concern. Chadwick had exposed the problem 40 years earlier (see pages 11-13) but now the inner cities were increasingly left to the poor as the middle classes moved to the growing suburbs. In the cities the building of main-line railway stations, large Victorian shopping streets and large department stores, led to demolition of many slums, but the poor were not compensated by new homes. In fact, needing to be close to their place of work, and only being able to afford low rents, they moved into nearby areas which were already overcrowded.

Housing and health

In 1884 and 1885 the Royal Commission of the Working Classes published its report.

The evils of overcrowding, especially in London, are still a public scandal, and are becoming in certain localities a worse scandal than they ever were. Among adults, overcrowding causes a vast amount of suffering which could be calculated by no bills of mortality, however accurate. The general deterioration in the health of the people is a worse feature of overcrowding than . . . infectious disease. It has the effect of reducing their stamina, and thus producing consumption and diseases arising from general debility of the system whereby life is shortened . . . . In Liverpool nearly one-fifth of the squalid houses where the poor live in the closest quarters are reported to be always infected, that is to say, the seat of infectious diseases.

List the types of suffering which might result from living in overcrowded conditions where every room in a large tenement house might be shared by at least one family.

White Horse Close, Edinburgh. An Edwardian postcard, showing how once wealthy houses can become slums.

What sort of health problems might affect people living in overcrowded conditions?

The Established Church (the Church of England) had been slow to respond to the industrial changes and the growth of the cities. In 1851 a religious census found that the majority of working people were not attending church. The Catholics and the Nonconformists were still in touch, but the Church of England had become a church attended by the respectable middle and upper classes where the working man felt inferior. However in the middle years of the century ideas began to change and Evangelical Christians began to take the Christian message to the poor and also help them, through such practical measures as distributing food and clothing and giving medical help.

Whatever the motives for help – Christian duty, a feeling of conscience and guilt by the comfortably off, or even a means of preventing revolution by maintaining stability, money and material help was generously given.

Martin Tupper (1810-89) in *The Homes of the Poor* expressed in verse popular feeling towards the poor.

Cleanliness, healthiness, water, and light,
Rent within reason, and temperate rules,
Work and fair wages (Humanity's right),
Libraries, hospitals, churches, and schools –
Thus, let us help the good brother in need,
Dropping a treasure at Industry's door,
Glad, by God's favour, to lighten indeed
The Burdens of life in the homes of the poor.

O! there is much to be done, and that soon;
Classes are standing asunder, aloof;
Hasten, Benevolence, with the free boon.
Falling as sunshine on Misery's roof!
Hasten, good stewards of a bountiful Lord,
Greatly to imitate Him evermore,

Binding together, in blessed accord,
The halls of the rich with the homes of the poor!

(*Source:* Quoted in D. Rubinstein, *Victorian Homes*, David and Charles, 1974)

What reasons does the poet put forward for helping the poor? Do you think the list in the first four lines covers all that was necessary to help the poor? Is the list still relevant today?

The Victorian response to the plight of the poor was considerable and a large number of charities were founded, taking up particular needs ranging from the provision of water for both animals and people (Metropolitan Drinking Fountain and Cattle Troughs Association) to Dr Barnardo's Homes (for destitute boys and girls). Each religious group had its own charitable organizations and it was during this period that many societies which still do much needed work were founded, such as the YMCA, the Salvation Army and the Shaftesbury Society. Each aimed to help those who could not help themselves, either in an institution such as a hospital or home, or by giving support for a particular purpose.

What was common to many of the charitable organizations was that they sought to provide help which would enable the recipient to improve his lot. Some would loan out mangles so that women could earn a living washing clothes. Others would teach a child a trade so that he might be apprenticed. Others provided housing on certain rigid conditions. Octavia Hill (1838-1912) was determined to improve the poor. In her housing schemes, the tenants had to conform to certain standards or they would be ejected. Education and improvement was the key.

I most heartily hope that whatever is done in building for the people may be done on a thoroughly sound commercial principle. I do not think it would help them the least in the long run to adopt any other principle; in fact, I believe it would be highly injurious to them . . . .

The people's homes are bad, partly because they are badly built and arranged; they are tenfold worse because the tenants' habits and lives are what they are. Transplant them tomorrow to healthy and commodious homes, and they would pollute and destroy them. They need, and will need for some time, a reformatory work which will demand that loving zeal of individuals which cannot be had for money, and cannot be legislated for by Parliament . . . . As soon as I entered into possession, each family had an opportunity of doing better: those who would not pay, or who led clearly immoral lives, were ejected. The rooms they vacated were cleansed; the tenants who showed signs of improvement moved into them, and thus, in turn, an opportunity was obtained for having each room distempered and painted . . . .

(*Source:* Octavia Hill, *Homes of the London Poor*, 1875)

The rent collectors were to be the educators and were carefully chosen and trained for their task. Do you think that this was a form of self help of which Samuel Smiles would have approved? Could it have been applied on a national scale?

THE GREAT DEPRESSION

The 1870s saw a succession of bad summers, leading to disease and poor crops. This coincided with competition from abroad especially from the North American prairie farmers benefitting from the new combine harvesters. With cheap transport they were able to export grain to Britain much more cheaply than Britain could produce it. In the next decade the refrigerated ship was introduced and farmers suffered as beef and lamb was imported from New Zealand and South America. In industry too, Britain increasingly became open to competition as the other nations began to catch up.

Joseph Chamberlain, the President of the Local Government Board, which was responsible for the Poor Law, was concerned at the plight of those who were not paupers, but "merely" poor.

To all Boards of Guardians

Local Government Board, Whitehall, S.W.

15th March, 1886

Sir,

The enquiries which have recently been undertaken by the Local Government Board unfortunately confirm the prevailing impression as to the existence of exceptional distress amongst the working classes. This distress is partial as to its locality, and is no doubt due in some measure to the long continued severity of the weather.

The returns of pauperism show an increase, but it is not yet considerable; and the numbers of persons in receipt of relief are greatly below those of previous periods of exceptional distress.

The Local Government Board have, however, thought it their duty to go beyond the returns of actual pauperism which are all that come under their notice in ordinary times, and they have made some investigation into the conditions of the working classes generally.

They are convinced that in the ranks of those who do not ordinarily seek poor law relief there is evidence of much and increasing privation, and if the depression in trade continues it is to be feared that large numbers of persons usually in regular employment will be reduced to the greatest straits.

. . . The spirit of independence which leads so many of the working classes to make great personal sacrifices rather than incur the stigma of pauperism, is one which deserves the greatest sympathy and respect.

(*Source: Pauperism and Distress: Circular Letter to Boards of Guardians*, 1886)

However Chamberlain was against any relaxation in the Poor Law test. On what grounds would he have argued against change? He then went on to advocate certain types of work for those who were temporarily unemployed.

1. Work which will not involve the stigma of pauperism.

2. Work which all can perform, whatever may have been their previous avocations; (jobs).

3. Work which does not compete with that of other labourers at present in employment.

4. Work which will not interfere with the resumption of regular employment in their trades by those who seek it.

(*Source: Pauperism and Distress . . .*, 1886)

Can you suggest what sort of work Chamberlain had in mind? Do you think that Chamberlain's attitude towards the poor has developed by contrast with those held by some in 1834?

In 1891 John A. Hobson in *The Problem of Poverty* wrote about the problems of the industrial poor and what society should do to solve the problem. He was particularly concerned with the danger of doing nothing.

So in England the change of industrial conditions which has massed the poor in great cities, the spread of knowledge by compulsory education, cheap newspapers, libraries, and a thousand other vehicles of knowledge, the possession and growing appreciation of political power, have made poverty more self conscious and the poor more discontented. By striving to educate, intellectually, morally, sanitarily, the poor, we have made them half-conscious of many needs they never recognised before . . . we have raised the standard of the requirements of a decent human life, but we have not increased to a corresponding degree their power to attain them . . . . The income of the poor has grown, but their desires and needs have grown more rapidly.

(*Source:* J.A. Hobson, *The Problem of Poverty*, Methuen, 1891)

Why was Hobson worried even though the income and possessions of the poor had risen?

THREE CASE STUDIES In the latter part of the century three men in their different ways brought the problems and the extent of poverty to the people at large. They were Charles Booth, William Booth (not related) and Seebohm Rowntree. Each had his findings published in books which had large sales, apart from providing numerous newspaper articles.

Charles Booth and the London Poor

Charles Booth spent over 20 years investigating the condition of the London poor. There had been many studies before but his was the first scientific study of such a large number of people. Together with a team of investigators he began with the East End which was known to be poor and found:

	Crowding	*Poverty*
Bethnal Green	55%	47%
Hoxton and Hagerston	51½%	41%
Old St. and S. Shoreditch	57%	48%
Gray's Inn and Clerkenwell	53½%	45%

An advertisement from Charles Booth's Life and Labour in London. *The series was very popular, but the prices are a clue to the readership.*

The crowding is in excess of 8 or 9 points in the percentage; rents here are high, and the standard of life very low.

He then turned his attention to the remainder of London and found poverty in varying degrees in every part:

	Crowding	*Poverty*
St. Margarets and Belgrave	55%	15½%
Mayfair and North of Hyde Park	23½%	14%
Brompton	12½%	5%

Crowding . . . undoubtedly connected with coachmen's quarters over their stables.

Why do you think that there is such a close link between overcrowding and poverty as shown in these figures?

In his conclusion to Volume II of the Poverty series he produced the following table:

				%	%
Classes A & B	(the very poor)	354,444	or 8.4	(In poverty)	
Classes C & D	(the poor)	938,293	or 22.3	30.7	
Classes E & F	comfortable working class including all servants	2,166,503	or 51.5	(In comfort) 69.3	

Classes G & H	"lower middle" "middle" and "upper classes"	749,930 4,209,170	or 17.8	(In comfort)

Inmates of institutions	99,830

4,309,000 (estimated population 1889)

(*Source:* All figures taken from C. Booth, *Life and Labour of the People in London*, Macmillan, 1902)

William Booth and the Salvation Army

William Booth founded the Salvation Army in 1878 after over a decade of mission work amongst the poor in London. Soon after Stanley had found Livingstone in "darkest Africa", Booth wrote *In Darkest England and the Way Out* (1890). In it he described the work of the Army in taking the Christian message to the poor and their appeal to temperance. This was the belief that drink led to, or made poverty worse. Many temperance societies tried to get people to sign "The Pledge" – a document in which they agreed not to drink alcohol. Much practical help was given in the form of workshops, cheap food stores, lodgings for those who would work and abstain from drink, emigration schemes and even an employment exchange.

What is Sold at the Food Depots

For a Child

	d.			d.
Soup ...... Per Basin	¼	Coffee or Cocoa .... per cup		¼
Soup ... With Bread	½	Coffee or Cocoa with Bread and Jam ..		½

(*Source:* William Booth, *In Darkest England and the Way Out*, Salvation Army, *1890)*

Seebohm Rowntree of York

Seebohm Rowntree was impressed by the investigations of Charles Booth and began a similar survey in York, where he was chairman of the chocolate firm. His aim was to see whether he would find as many in poverty in York as Booth had done in London. He also employed researchers but in addition employed dieticians and physiologists so that he could study the nutritional value of the diets and their effect upon health and physique. In his study he divided poverty into two distinct types, primary and secondary.

1. Families whose total earnings are insufficient to obtain the minimum necessaries for the maintenance of merely physical efficiency. Poverty falling under this head may be described as "Primary" poverty.

2. Families whose total earnings would be sufficient for the maintenance of merely physical efficiency were it not that some portion of it is

Part of an illustration from William Booth's In Darkest England and the Way Out *(1890). Identify the major evils which Booth sought to remedy.*

absorbed by other expenditure either useful or wasteful. Poverty falling under this head may be described as "secondary" poverty.

Examples of secondary poverty were inability to spend money wisely through drink, gambling, smoking, etc.

	Numbers	% of total population of York	% of wages earning class
Persons in primary poverty	7,230	9.91	
Persons in secondary poverty	13,072	17.93	
Total number in poverty	20,302	27.84	43.4

Rowntree published his findings in *Poverty, A Study of Town Life* and they had a considerable impact for he had shown that London was not an exception and that if deep pockets of poverty were to be found in York, then they would probably be found in every area of the country.

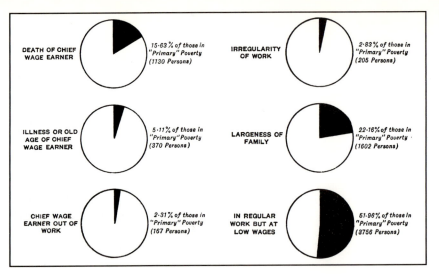

Rowntree's conclusion set the agenda for reformers in the twentieth century.

As the investigation into the conditions of life in this typical provincial town has proceeded, the writer has been increasingly impressed with the gravity of the facts which have unfolded themselves.

That in this land of abounding wealth, during a time of perhaps unexampled prosperity, probably more than one-fourth of the population are living in poverty, is a fact which may well cause great searchings of heart. There is surely need for a greater concentration of thought by the nation upon the well-being of its own people, for no civilization can be sound or stable which has at its base this mass of stunted human life.

... The object of the writer, however, has been to state facts rather than to suggest remedies. He desires, nevertheless, to express his belief that however difficult the path of social progress may be, a way of advance will open out before patient and penetrating thought if inspired by a true human sympathy.

(*Source:* B.S. Rowntree, *Poverty. A Study of Town Life*, Macmillan, 1901)

Significantly, what he did reject was the Malthusian idea which had led to the Poor Law Amendment Act of 1834. However it was to be a further 30 years before the workhouse system was finally ended.

ON REFLECTION:

How important do you think religion was in seeking to bring about improvement?

What effects do you think the increasing literacy of the working people would have had? Do you think it would have made them more dissatisfied or given them the skills to improve themselves?

Liberal Social Policy 1906–1914

In the election of January 1906, 401 Liberal MPs were returned, whilst the number of Conservatives fell from 402 to 157 giving the Liberals a majority of 356. (They were supported by 29 Labour and 32 Irish Nationalists.)

The period of Liberal Government between 1906 and 1914 was to see several important social reforms, so significant that some historians have seen them as laying the foundation of the Welfare State which was to be consolidated by further reforms after the Second World War.

Strangely, the Liberals were not returned on an election platform of social reform, but there were good reasons why, with a particular combination of personalities, such as Lloyd George and Churchill, change should occur at this time.

COPYRIGHT. R. HAINES. RT. HON. D. LLOYD GEORGE. 487.A. BEAGLES POSTCARDS.

An Edwardian postcard of David Lloyd George. Is the fact that he was the subject of a postcard significant?

Apart from the evidence discussed in the previous chapter which showed the extent of poverty throughout Britain, there were several other reasons why the time was ripe for reform.

The Second Boer War (1899-1902) and the National Efficiency Campaign

The war against the two small Boer Republics in Southern Africa had eventually been won, but it had taken much longer than anticipated and furthermore some 25% of the volunteers for military service were physically below the required standard. A Royal Commission in Scotland on Physical Training reported in 1903 that there had been a national deterioration (decline) amongst children and recommended the introduction of school meals. In the following year an Interdepartmental Committee on Physical Deterioration recommended medical inspection and school meals in schools run by local authorities. However, the recommendations were not acted upon because of the Conservative fear of raising either national taxes, or local rates, to pay for the reforms. Nevertheless, by 1905 there was a widespread feeling in Britain that our national efficiency was at stake and that the government had to introduce social reform in order to make the country's children more healthy, so that in time they would become healthier workers and soldiers in case of war. This belief that the nation was falling behind and that something must be done, was increased by the rise of the USA and Germany as great industrial powers and competitors.

Collectivism

Sidney Webb was a Fabian Socialist and a prolific writer on social problems. He hoped that eventually the State would take a greater responsibility for the individual, and that this would be achieved by various acts of Parliament. This belief is known as collectivism. Here, Webb argues that there was already more intervention than many thought:

The practical man, oblivious or contemptuous of any theory of the social organism or general principles of social organisation, has been forced, by the necessities of the time, into an ever-deepening collectivist channel. Socialism, of course, he still rejects and despises. The individualist town councillor will walk along the municipal pavement, lit by municipal gas, and cleansed by municipal brooks with municipal water, and seeing, by the municipal clock in the municipal market, that he is too early to meet his children coming from the municipal school, hard by the county lunatic asylum and municipal hospital, will use the national telegraph system to tell them not to walk through the municipal park, but to come by the municipal tramway, to meet him in the municipal reading-room, by the municipal art gallery, museum, and library, where he intends to consult some of the national publications in order to prepare his next speech in the municipal town hall, in favour of the nationalisation of canals and the increase of Government control over the railway system. 'Socialism, Sir,' he will say, 'don't waste the time of a practical man by your fantastic

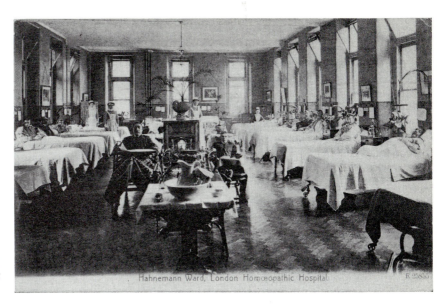

Hahnemann Ward,
London Homoeopathic
Hospital, 1905.

absurdities. Self-help, Sir, individual self-help, that's what's made our city what it is'.

(*Source:* Sidney Webb, *Socialism in England*, 1890)

List the ways in which Webb shows that the town or city had already taken over and was already organizing areas of local concern. What point is Webb making in the last four lines?

Nevertheless there was to be much resistance, as the following article in *The Times* of 2 January 1905 illustrates, in challenging the conclusions of the Committee on Physical Deterioration.

We have already made a serious inroad upon personal independence by relieving parents of the duty of educating their children. That is now used as an argument for relieving them of the duty of feeding their children. When we have done that, the argument will be stronger than ever for relieving them of the duty of clothing their children. It will be said that we pay vast sums for teaching and feeding, but that the money is wasted if the children are not properly clad .... From that it is an easy step to paying for their proper housing; for what, it will be asked, is the use of feeding, clothing, and teaching children, if they come to school from close and insanitary bed-rooms? ... The proposed measure would go far to sap the remaining independence of the existing parents; but what are we to expect from the present children when they in turn become parents? The habit of looking to the State for their maintenance would be ingrained in them; everything we now give would be to them a matter of course; and they would infallibly make new demands of their own.

(*Source: The Times*, 2 January 1905)

What are the main dangers of giving help as seen by The Times*?*

Political motives

David Lloyd George and Winston Churchill both came to play an increasingly important part in the Liberal Party. They came to represent what was known as the "New Liberalism", those to the left of the party, who wished to press forward with a programme of social reform. Their motives were both humanitarian and political.

Lloyd George in a speech given at Cardiff in October 1906 argued that the Labour Party would only prove a serious threat if the Liberals failed

to cope seriously with the social conditions of the people, to remove the national degradation of slums and widespread poverty in a land glittering with wealth.

(*Source:* D. Lloyd George, *Better Times*, 1910)

Furthermore, both Lloyd George and Churchill believed in the existing economic structure (capitalism) and did not wish to see it overthrown. They argued that it was better to improve the system by preventing further class antagonism.

THE LIBERAL PARTY REFORMS

For children

In spite of *The Times'* warning, the Liberals introduced free school meals for the poor to be paid for out of the rates. Significantly, the parents did not have to be classified as paupers, and thus we have the first example of aid outside the Poor Law. In the following year in 1907 health inspection and school clinics were introduced.

The Bradford Local Education Authority, which fixed the charge at 2d, prepared a list of 17 dinners, each of two courses. A week's dietary is given as a specimen:

Monday	Lentil and tomato soup. Currant roly-poly pudding.
Tuesday	Meat pudding (stewed beef and boiled suet pudding). Ground-rice pudding.
Wednesday	Yorkshire pudding, gravy, peas. Rice and sultanas.
Thursday	Scotch barley broth. Currant pastry or fruit tart.
Friday	Stewed fish, parsley sauce, peas, mashed potatoes. Cornflour blancmange. All these meals included bread.

(*Source:* Quoted in E. Royston Pike, *Human Documents of the Lloyd George Era*, Allen & Unwin, 1972)

What is the great advantage for the child of providing a free school meal?

The Children's Act, 1908

Its aim was to protect the child and it now became a legal offence for parents to neglect the health of their children. In addition children were no longer to be sent to prison if they were under the age of 14. Young offenders were to be sent to Borstal (named after a village in Kent where the first one was built). Also children were to be kept in remand homes before the trial which was now to be held in a Juvenile Court.

Old age pensions 1908

By 1908 the issue of pensions for the old was no longer controversial. Charles Booth had recommended them as a result of his survey amongst the London poor. In addition Joseph Chamberlain had in the 1890s sought to introduce them during Lord Salisbury's Conservative administration. Germany, Britain's leading European competitor, had introduced a scheme of Old Age Pensions and Social Insurance in the 1880s, and New Zealand had done so in 1899. The problems in Britain were whether the scheme should be contributory or non-contributory, and also the age at which a person would be able to receive a pension, and lastly the cost of the scheme. The discussion had been postponed during the Boer War.

Lloyd George, the newly appointed Chancellor of the Exchequer in Asquith's Government in 1908, had no doubt that pensions should be introduced, for both political and social reasons.

A Punch cartoon, August 1908. Why is Lloyd George portrayed as a highwayman?

THE PHILANTHROPIC HIGHWAYMAN.

Mr. Lloyd George. *"I'LL MAKE 'EM PITY THE AGED POOR!"*

It is time we did something that appealed straight to the people – it will, I think, help to stop this electoral rot and that is most necessary.

(*Source:* Lloyd George in a letter to his brother. Quoted in D. Fraser, *The Evolution of the Welfare State*, Macmillan, 1978)

The Liberals had lost seats in recent by-elections to the Labour Party.

In the same year Lloyd George made a speech at Manchester in which he said:

The task is great and it is difficult. The task of every reformer is heart-breaking. There are sympathies to arouse, there are suspicions to allay. There are hopes to excite, there are fears to calm. There are faint hearts to sustain, there are hot heads to restrain. There is the dormant interest in right to wake up, there is many a vested interest in wrong to be beaten down. . . .

If these poor people are to be redeemed they must be redeemed not by themselves, because nothing strikes you more than the stupor of despair in which they have sunk – they must be redeemed by others outside, and the appeal ought to be to every class of the community to see that in this great land all this misery and wretchedness should be put an end to.

(*Source:* Quoted in H. du Parcq, *Life of David Lloyd George*, Caxton, 1913)

What does Lloyd George see as the main problems faced by the reformer? Why does he believe that the poor need outside help? What motive for reforms have we in the letter which is not present in the speech? Why is this?

The Pension Bill was introduced in 1908. The Pension was to be non-contributory and paid of right to those over 70. The amount of 5 shillings was not generous, but the precedent was set for further increases. The response was far greater than anticipated and Lloyd George explained the large number of applications by the fact that there was

A mass of poverty and destitution which is too proud to wear the badge of pauperism.

(*Source:* quoted in H. du Parcq, *Life of David Lloyd George*)

In other words, the Poor Law had worked too well in acting as a deterrent to the proud, even though they may have been old and in need. The new measure was important because it was paid for out of taxation and was also to be given by right.

Flora Thompson who was then a village postmistress in rural Oxfordshire described the response in her book:

When . . . the Old Age Pensions began, life was transformed for such aged cottagers. They were relieved of anxiety. They were suddenly rich. Independent for life! At first when they went to the Post Office to draw it, tears of gratitude would run down the cheeks of some, and they would say as they picked up their money, "God bless that Lord George!" (for they could not believe that one so powerful and munificent could be a plain "Mr") and "God bless you, miss!" and there were flowers from their gardens and apples from their trees for the girl who merely handed them the money.

(*Source:* Flora Thompson, *Lark Rise*, OUP, 1939)

Why were the old so grateful, even though the amount was so small?

The Royal Commission on the Poor Laws and the Relief of Distress, 1905-9

This had been set up by the Conservative leader Arthur Balfour on the day he resigned from office in December 1905. The Report of 1909 illustrated the deep divisions which existed as to what should be done with the Poor Law system, which was still essentially the same as that established in 1834.

The Majority Report recommended that the administration of the Poor Law should be transferred to local government, so that it would come under the control of the County and County Borough Councils. In other words they wished both to reform and retain the Poor Law. They also stressed:

that every effort should be made to foster the instinct of independence and self maintenance amongst those assisted.

Mr J.S. Davy, head of the Poor Law Division, put it more strongly:

man must stand by his accidents, he must suffer for the general good of the body politic (i.e. the whole).

The authors of the Minority Report argued quite differently

We have seen that it is not practicable to oust the various specialised Local Authorities that have grown up since the Boards of Guardians were established. There remains only the alternative – to which, indeed, the conclusions of each of our chapters seem to us to point – of completing the process of breaking up the Poor Law, which has been going on for the last three decades.

(*Source: Minority Report*, 1909)

Sidney Webb, who had drafted the Minority Report, wrote that

The minority commissioners, however, after a more extensive and searching investigation than had ever before been undertaken, came to the conclusion that unemployment was mainly due to defects of industrial organisation which it is fully in the power of the state to remedy, if and when it chooses. As a consequence of this new knowledge we are now as a nation morally responsible for the continued existence of the great army

A postcard of 1909. Note the benefits paid, and the contributions.

of 'out-of-works' in our midst in a far more direct and unmistakeable sense than ever before.

(*Source:* From an article in *The Crusade*, January 1911, quoted in R.C. Birch, *The Shaping of the Welfare State*, Longman, 1976)

The Poor Law was not ended until 1929. Do the above views give an indication as to why the issue was not resolved in 1909?

THE 1909 BUDGET

Lloyd George and Churchill did not wish to get too far ahead of the Liberal Party and so favoured dealing with the effects of such industrial problems as unemployment, rather than attempting to cure the causes. Old age pensions had cost more than anticipated, and if further reforms were to be introduced, more money had to be raised. Money was also needed for the improvement of the Royal Navy, and in particular a Dreadnought programme.

The rejection of the Budget by the House of Lords led to a constitutional crisis only resolved by the Parliament Act of 1911 which reduced the powers of the Upper Chamber. Lloyd George had not set out to break the House of Lords, but several of his tax measures, such as the land tax and the death tax, led to an attack on him and he reacted in kind.

. . . a fully-equipped duke costs as much to keep up as two "Dreadnoughts", and they are just as great a terror, and they last longer . . . I wonder how many people there are who realise what gigantic powers those who own the land possess upon the life of the nation?

(*Source:* Lloyd George at Newcastle, 1909)

Asquith, the Prime Minister, expressed the Liberal aims in a more moderate manner:

Sickness, invalidity, unemployment – these are spectres which are always hovering on the horizon of possibility, I may almost say of certainty, to the industrious workman. We believe here also the time has come for the State to lend a helping hand. That is the secret, or at least it is one of the secrets, of the Budget of this year . . . it was a Budget which sought by taxes on the accumulations of the rich and the luxuries of the well-to-do, and by a moderate toll on monopoly values which the community itself has, either actively or passively, created, to provide the sinews of war for the initiation and the prosecution of what must be a long, a costly, social campaign. That was the Budget put forward on the authority of a United Cabinet – passed after months of by no means fruitless discussion by the House of Commons – rejected in a week, and at a single blow, by the House of Lords. And that, gentlemen, is primarily why we are here to-night.

(*Source:* Speech at the Albert Hall, quoted in *The Times*, 11 December 1909)

Why do you think that Asquith speaks of the spectres for the "industrious" workmen and not merely the workmen? In which sentence is he giving support to his Chancellor?

THE NATIONAL INSURANCE ACT, 1911

Lloyd George saw National Insurance for the sick and unemployment as a logical extension of the Old Age Pension Act. He believed in

provisions against the accidents of life which bring so much undeserved poverty to hundreds of thousands of homes, accidents which are quite inevitable such as the death of the breadwinner or his premature breakdown in health. I have always thought that the poverty which was brought upon families owing to these causes presents a much more urgent demand upon the practical sympathy of the community than even Old Age Pensions. With old age the suffering is confined to the individual alone; but in these other cases it extends to the whole family of the victim of circumstances.

(*Source:* Quoted in D. Fraser, *Evolution of the British Welfare State*)

Why does Lloyd George believe that National Insurance is so important?

Although Lloyd George accepted the need, he accepted that because of cost, it could not be non-contributory. However, the Webbs believed that a compulsory scheme would be doomed to failure.

Any attempt to *enforce* on people of this country – whether for supplementary pensions, provision for sickness or invalidity, or anything else – a system of direct, personal, weekly contribution must, in our judgment, in face of so powerful a phalanx as the combined Friendly Societies, Trade Unions and Industrial Insurance Companies, fighting in defence of their own business, prove politically disastrous.

(*Source:* Minority Report on the Poor Law, 1909)

Why would each of the groups named be against a compulsory Government scheme?

Political motives, as always, were strong in the minds of Lloyd George and Churchill, though this is not to doubt their sincerity. Nevertheless, the efforts needed to get through what Lloyd George called his "ambulance wagon" were enormous. Consequently the Act reflected the compromises which had to be made. One of Lloyd George's talents was an awareness of the dangers.

. . . one would have to encounter the bitter hostility of powerful organisations like the Prudential, the Liver, the Royal Victoria, the Pearl and similar institutions with an army numbering scores if not hundreds of thousands of agents and collectors who make a living out of collecting a few pence a week from millions of households . . . they visit every house, they are indefatigable, they are often very intelligent and a Government which attempted to take over their work without first of all securing the co-operation of the other party would inevitably fail in its undertaking.

(*Source:* Extract from the Lloyd George Papers, quoted in D. Fraser, *Evolution of the Welfare State*)

The National Insurance Act was divided into two parts. The first dealt with Medical Insurance which gave up to 10 shillings a week for 26 weeks, plus free medical treatment. The new Insurance Commission was to pay the doctor a fee, for his "panel" patients, and he could still continue to have private fee-paying patients.

Payment was to be by contributions of 4d a week by the worker, 3d from the employer and 2d from the State. Lloyd George sold the idea as giving 9d for 4d. The scheme was to be administered by certain approved societies.

Explain how Lloyd George won over the "powerful organizations".

Part II of the Act dealt with Unemployment Insurance. At first this was restricted to certain industries which were liable to heavy seasonal unemployment. The payments were 2½d for the worker, 2½d from the employer and 1²⁄₃d from the state. The payments were only payable to those who had contributed to the scheme.

Lloyd George summed it up as follows in a speech at Kennington, London in 1912:

So long as the head of the family is in good health, on the whole with a

THE PITILESS PHILANTHROPIST.

Mr. Lloyd George: "NOW UNDERSTAND, I'VE BROUGHT YOU OUT TO DO YOU GOOD,
AND GOOD I WILL DO YOU, WHETHER YOU LIKE IT OR NOT."

fierce struggle he can keep the wolves of hunger in the vast majority of
cases from the door; but when he breaks down in health, his children are
at the mercy of these fierce ravaging beasts, and there is no one there to
stand at the door to fight for the young. What happens in these cases? In
hundreds of thousands there is penury, privation, everything going from
the household, nothing left unpawned, except its pride. On Monday next
an Act of Parliament comes into operation that abolishes that state of
things for ever. Twenty-seven millions of money raised as a fund – raised
as a parapet between the people and the poverty that comes from sickness
and unemployment!

(*Source:* Quoted in H. Du Parcq, *Life of David Lloyd George*)

*Why does Lloyd George believe that National Insurance is so important for
the whole family, not just for the individual? Imagine you are a building
worker, unemployed for the winter of 1909, and also in the winter of 1914.
Try writing some extracts from a diary for those times, thinking about the
importance of the Act to an unemployed person.*

OPPOSITION TO THE ACT

On 30 November 1911, *The Times* reported on a meeting held at the Albert
Hall. It had been called by those who employed domestic servants and now
as employers would have to pay for a weekly stamp.

They were met to fight the battle of the small householder, the battle of
the rank and file of servants, the battle of the socially, physically, or

mentally handicapped. Small householders called upon to pay 26s. a year for the servants they employed, would either have to take the amount out of their wages or do without them. In either case the poorer of the two parties, the maid, would suffer most . . . .

By what right did Mr. Lloyd George decree that every mistress was to be a tax-gatherer? Not only had she to collect his tax, but she had to decide on whose shoulders that tax should fall, with a moral, but no legal power to enforce her decisions.

(*Source: The Times*, 30 November 1911)

Philip Snowden speaking in the House of Commons on the National Insurance Bill, 1911

The practice of requiring a direct contribution for social services has been gradually abandoned during the last thirty years, because it was both expensive and ineffective. I submit working people cannot afford to pay the contribution which is to be exacted from them under this Bill . . . .

My second objection was that it is irritating and cumbersome. I am quite sure if this Bill passes into law the compulsory deduction every week from the wages of workmen will be very much resented . . . . The case I shall attempt to put against a direct contribution of the employer is because I feel it will prove disastrous to working men themselves. I really cannot imagine any sensible reason why an employer should be called upon to make a direct contribution for the support of his sick work people during times of sickness.

(*Source:* Quoted by D. Read, *Documents from Edwardian England*, Harrap, 1973)

Snowden supported a non-contributory scheme because he felt that it was wrong to make everyone contribute the same amount. He was a socialist and believed that the burden should fall on the whole community through national taxation. What did he fear the employer would do to keep his/her costs down?

ON REFLECTION:

There is much controversy over the importance of the Liberal Reforms and how far they laid the foundations of the Welfare State. Which of the reforms do you think was the most important? Why? Consider how much of what was introduced was already available under the Poor Law. The reforms were very important because they enabled the individual who was in real need to seek help by right, without the social stigma of the Poor Law.

The Inter War Years 1919–1939

THE EFFECTS OF THE FIRST WORLD WAR

The First World War was the first total war. That is a war which saw the total involvement of both those fighting in the armed forces, and those civilians at home. The war saw a rethinking of many liberal values, and an involvement by the State which would have been unthought of in 1914. With the shortage of men and the need for more control, voluntary recruitment gave way to conscription for all those over 19 in 1916. By the end of the war rationing, identity cards and various non-strike agreements had been introduced. In addition the Government came to control and direct the major industries so that the war effort could be better pursued. To this end the mines were nationalized.

Thus the old idea of laissez-faire was swept away. Lloyd George, when he became Prime Minister of the Coalition Government in December 1916, introduced measures which he ironically dubbed "War Socialism".

Equally the enormity of the sacrifice, with nearly every family suffering in

The war led to rationing and restrictions, as shown in this contemporary postcard.

Everyone during the war had to be registered. In 1915 my father volunteered.

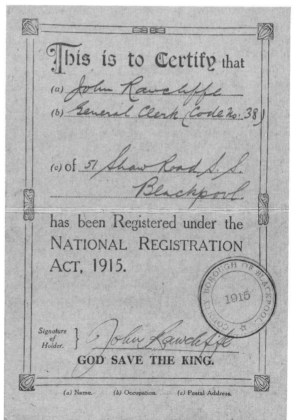

some way, led to rising hopes for the future, when victory was finally achieved.

In 1917 a Ministry of Reconstruction was formed headed by Dr Christopher Addison. The War Cabinet's view of reconstruction was that "it was not so much a question of rebuilding society as it was before the war, but of moulding a better world out of the social and economic conditions which have come into being during the war".

Lloyd George was well aware of the needs (some 1 in 3 of the conscripts were unfit for military service). Speaking to labour leaders he said;

> The present war . . . presents an opportunity for reconstruction of industrial and economic conditions of this country such as has never been presented in the life of, probably, the world. The whole state of society is more or less molten and you can stamp upon that molten mass almost anything so long as you do it with firmness and determination . . . . The country will be prepared for bigger things immediately after the war . . . will be in a more enthusiastic mood, in a more exalted mood for the time being – in a greater mood for doing big things; and unless the opportunity is seized immediately after the war I believe it will pass away . . . .
>
> (*Source:* Quoted in B.B. Gilbert, *British Social Policy 1914-39*, Batsford 1970)

Politicians were also aware of the dangers if hopes were not realized. The successful Bolshevik revolution in Russia in November 1917 affected thinking at home, especially when strikes began to break out again in 1919. Thus health, housing and education and unemployment were all high on the post war agenda for a variety of reasons.

HOUSING The beginning of the war in 1914 had led to an end in house building and by 1918 it was estimated that the country was 600,000 houses short. In the election of 1918 Lloyd George called for "Homes for Heroes", and to this end the Housing and Town Planning Act of 1919 was introduced by Addison, the Minister of Health. In the Autumn of 1919 the Directorate of Intelligence reported

> The need for houses grows more acute as the weather grows colder. The unrest caused by lack of houses cannot be exaggerated: it is further accentuated by evictions and by the erection in certain districts of Kinematograph Theatres instead of houses. The unrest caused by the housing space difficulties has frequently been alluded to in my reports: it is certainly increasing. In fact there is probably no more active cause of discontent than this. There is an outcry against the proposal to legalize increased rents, and my correspondent at Leeds states that if rents are raised there will be extensive 'rent strikes'.
>
> (*Source:* Quoted by B.B. Gilbert, *British Social Policy*)

Clearly the Government saw the need for house building. How did reports such as this bring extra pressure on them to act quickly?

Under the Housing Act, local authorities were obliged to fulfil the need for houses and in the next two years 213,000 new houses were built,

A bye-law was introduced in Manchester insisting that houses must be at least 30 feet (9.15 m) apart. Here you can see one street before the bye-law was enforced, and another in 1870 after the bye-law took effect.

stimulated by Government subsidies to local councils and to private builders. However by 1921 there were high land prices and high interest rates and the initiative was to be brought to an end in that year when Addison was dismissed and economies were introduced. In fact rising costs had meant that houses which were built for £250 in 1914 had risen to £1,250 in 1919.

After the Conservatives withdrew from the Coalition in 1922 and Lloyd George was forced to resign, two-party government returned. With the Conservatives in power for the first time since 1905, Neville Chamberlain became Minister of Health and in March 1923 he introduced a second Housing Act. This time the emphasis was on the private builder who was given £6 for every house built for the next 20 years. The following year saw the first minority Labour Government and the new Minister of Health, John Wheatley, introduced a third Housing Act which increased the subsidy to £9, not only to private builders but also to local authorities. This scheme led to over half a million houses being built.

Look at the following figures and the extract which follows and consider the achievements in housing between 1919 and 1939 and also try to identify the continuing problems.

i. 1918-39 4m. houses built
1930-39 Local authorities built 273,000 houses
1930-39 Local authorities demolished 242,000 houses.

ii. *Analysis of overcrowding in 26 sublet houses in – Street, Somer's Town, N.W.1.* (The street contains 30 houses, 4 of which are occupied by, as they were built for, one family, and are therefore excluded from the table):

No. of houses 26
No. of rooms 158
No. of families 88
Average no. of families per house 3.4
    Maximum no. of families per house 5
    Minimum   – ditto –   2

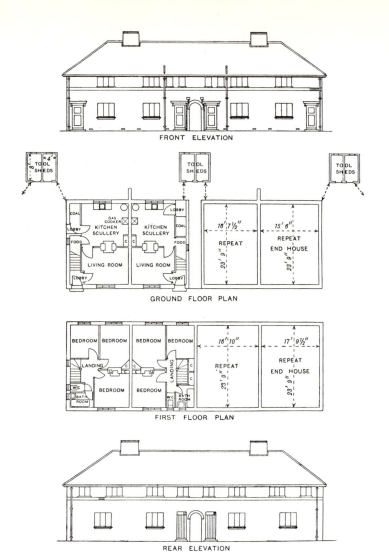

FRONT ELEVATION

TOOL SHEDS

KITCHEN SCULLERY

KITCHEN SCULLERY

LIVING ROOM

LIVING ROOM

GROUND FLOOR PLAN

BEDROOM BEDROOM BEDROOM BEDROOM

LANDING

LANDING

BEDROOM BEDROOM

FIRST FLOOR PLAN

REAR ELEVATION

Plan of an inter-war council house. List the ways in which this is an improvement on earlier inner city housing.

Total no. of persons 417
No. of persons over 14 262
No. of persons under 14 155
Average no. of rooms per family 1.8
Average no. of persons per room 2.6

No. of families overcrowded:
1. On the Registrar-General's standard   41 or 46.5 per cent
2. On standard of 2.5 persons per bedroom   28 or 31.8 per cent
3. On standard of separation of sexes   14 or 15.9 per cent

iii.

The Medical Officer of Health of Canlachie (Glasgow) in his report for 1927, stated that "In the Northern Division there were several single-room houses with 13 people in back room, and in one two-roomed house in the South-Western Division there were 29 people".

(*Source:* ii. and iii. quoted from E.D. Simon, *How to Abolish the Slums*, Longman, 1929)

The beginning of the Downham Estate in the early 1930s. It was built on the Bromley/Lewisham borders for many families from Bermondsey and south London.

UNEMPLOYMENT

Between 1921 and 1938 those without work never fell below 10 per cent and at its peak in 1932 over one in five of the population was unemployed. Economically our old heavy industries were in decline, especially coal, cotton and ship building. These industries were hit by foreign competition and the fact that they were no longer competitive, often working with old, outdated machinery.

At the same time some of the newer industries flourished. The car and electrical industries and house building all flourished. This affected the regions differently. Thus London and South Eastern England, with a rising population, flourished whilst areas such as East Lancashire and the North East suffered badly, with high rates of unemployment.

The Unemployment Insurance Act, 1911, had assumed an unemployment rate of no more than 8.5 per cent amongst qualified

An industrial photograph from the early 1920s. Note the chimneys and pottery kilns.

FRESH AIR FOR THE POTTERIES.

S.I.

workers. In 1918 an unemployment donation was introduced in order to avoid discontent amongst returning troops who might find themselves without work. By this measure the unemployed had the right to be paid 24 shillings for 13 weeks, if there was no work.

In 1920 the Unemployment Act was passed. It gave benefit to all manufacturing workers earning less than £250 a year, at the rate of 15 shillings per week for 15 weeks. However by this time there were 1.5 million unemployed and by 1921 the fund was exhausted.

Extract from Report on Revolutionary Organizations, 1920

Marches of the unemployed are frequent and although they are often made up of men who do not want work, the Communist party are gaining many recruits, while the meetings of patriotic societies are continually broken up. I have received specimens of the kind of speeches delivered by Communist agitators. They are all directed toward exciting class hatred. 'When', they say, 'are you going to begin? This is going to be a black and terrible winter for the workers; millions now will be thrown out of work. You will be forced to take action before long, or starve. Why wait? Why not begin now? Use the power that is in your hands', etc., etc.

(*Source:* Quoted in B.B. Gilbert, *British Social Policy*)

How might reports such as this have influenced the Government into introducing measures to help the unemployed?

The result was that the insurance part of the scheme failed, because the insurance fund soon fell into a deficit. This was made worse because many people were seeking help from the insurance fund rather than the Poor Law. This money, or extended or uncovenanted benefit, became popularly known as the dole, and was the individual's safeguard against the workhouse. Its weakness was that the Government had not planned the system and had simply responded to mass unemployment. When the Labour Party came to power in 1924, it raised the dole to 18 shillings.

By this time unemployment was down to 10 per cent but in the areas of old heavy industry the figures were different.

1923/4	Shipbuilding and repairing	28% unemployment
	Cotton	16% unemployment
	Engineering, iron and steel	14.5% unemployment
	Cars	8.0% unemployment

J.B. Priestley, the novelist, toured England in 1933 and commented on the contrasts between the regions.

There was, first, old England, the country of the cathedrals and minsters and manor houses and inns, of Parson and Squire; guide-book and quaint highways and byways England .... Then, I decided, there is the nineteenth-century England, the industrial England of coal, iron, steel, cotton, wool, railways; of thousands of rows of little houses all alike, sham Gothic churches, square-faced chapels, Town Halls, Mechanics'

CONTRIBUTION 1s. 6d. a week. Date of entry into Insurance if after 5th July, 1929. 7/11/27	RECORD OF CONTRIBUTIONS.										
	Contribution Year ending 3rd July, 1932, governing Benefit Year 1933.		Contribution Year ending 2nd July, 1933, governing Benefit Year 1934.		Contribution Year ending 1st July, 1934, governing Benefit Year 1935.		Contribution Year ending 7th July, 1935, (53 weeks) governing Benefit Year 1936.		Contribution Year ending 5th July, 1936, governing Benefit Year 1937.	
	Number of Contributions.	Initials of Society Official.	Number of Contributions.	Initials of Society Official.	Number of Contributions.	Initials of Society Official.	Number of Contributions.	Initials of Society Official.	Number of Contributions.	Initials of Society Official.
CONTRIBUTIONS PAID {July to Dec.	31 11	aftm	33 2	atm	33 —	—	34		35	
{Jan. to June	32 6	aftm	33 llrv	fr	34		35		36	
CONTRIBUTIONS ALLOWED. (a) for notified incapacity or weeks before Insce. began, &c.										
(b) on account of proved unemployment ...	F.15 F 20	aftm aftm	F 24 F 26.	aftm fr	F 3	mfy				
TOTAL CREDITED ...	17	aftm	2.	fr						
ARREARS DUE			23 @ 9	fr						
ARREARS PAID ...			23 @ 9	fr						

EFFECT OF ARREARS ON HEALTH INSURANCE BENEFITS.

PENSIONS BENEFITS.
The conditions governing title to contributory pensions will be found in Leaflet W. P. & G. (Widows' and Orphans' Pensions) and Leaflet O.A.P. 107 G (Old Age Pensions). Copies of these Leaflets may be obtained at any Post Office.
Application for old age pension may be made at any time within four months before the applicant's 65th birthday.

1. The health insurance benefits payable to you during a Benefit Year (which begins on the first Monday in January) depend upon the number of contributions credited to you for the Contribution Year ended in the previous July.
2. If any arrears for a Contribution Year are due from you, your health insurance benefits will be reduced or suspended during the next Benefit Year unless you make up the arrears within the period of grace (which runs from the end of the contribution year to the 30th November).
3. Particulars of the arrears due for any contribution year should be notified to you by your Society by means of an Arrears Notice, and the notice will set out the amount of the requisite arrears payment, the manner in which it should be made, and the effect upon your benefits if you pay only part of the arrears.
4. If, for any Contribution Year, arrears are due, but no Arrears Notice has reached you by the 1st October following, you should ask your Society for one.

TERMINATION OF INSURANCE.
A person remains in insurance for only a limited time after his employment has ceased, whether or not he has paid arrears. A person who has ceased to be insurably employed and who desires to maintain his insurance and benefit rights should keep in touch with his Approved Society, and ascertain what he requires to do, and as to becoming a Voluntary Contributor, if necessary, in order to avoid cessation of insurance. Memorandum 247/X, which gives information regarding termination of insurance, may be obtained from the Society.

A National Health and Pensions Insurance contribution card, begun in 1927 by a worker who contributed at the rate of 1/6d a week.

Institutes, mills, foundries, warehouses . . . a cynically devastated country-side, sooty dismal little towns, and still sootier grim fortress-like cities. This England makes up the larger part of the Midlands and the North and exists everywhere; but it is not being added to and has no new life poured into it . . . . The third England, I concluded, was the new post-war England, belonging far more to the age itself than to this particular island. America, I supposed, was its real birth-place. This is the England of arterial and by-pass roads, of filling stations and factories that look like exhibition buildings, of giant cinemas and dance-halls and cafes, bungalows with tiny garages, cocktail bars, Woolworths, motor-coaches, wireless, hiking, factory girls looking like actresses . . . .

(*Source:* J.B. Priestley, *English Journey*, Heinemann/Gollancz, 1934; Penguin, 1977)

How far does this description support the figures of unemployed? Into which category would you put the area where you live now? Try and find out what it was like in the 1930s.

By this time the Great Depression had bitten hard and in the 1930s unemployment insurance which had been designed to deal with short term unemployment now had to cope with those who had little prospect of ever finding work. These long-term unemployed accounted for one-third of all those on assistance.

Under the 1934 Unemployment Act the Government extended compulsory insurance, but gave nothing after 26 weeks. The scheme was intended to be self-supporting, out of contributions. Part II of the Act placed those who were without insurance benefit in the responsibility of the Unemployment Assistance Board, which gave benefits according to need. Relief was now to be on a national basis and in many ways marked the end of the Poor Law, although it still maintained responsibility for the old, the young and the sick.

In 1937 a report described the Poor Law

... as the other public social services have grown up and have relieved the Poor Law authorities of some part of their burden, the Poor Law itself has mellowed and become more expansive. Instead of the grim Poor Law of the 19th century with its rigorous insistence on the principle of "less eligibility" and the workhouse test we have a liberal and constructive service supplementing the other social services, filling in gaps and dealing with human need in the round in a way which no specialist service could ever be expected to do.

(*Source:* Report on the Social Services, quoted in D. Fraser, *The Evolution of the British Welfare State*)

The Workhouse Test had been ended in 1930. How had the 1934 Act helped to make the Poor Law less harsh? Are there any other reasons which had led to this change of attitude?

THE END OF THE POOR LAW

The view of the Royal Commission on the Poor Law which had reported in 1909 had been that unemployment was a disease and the Unemployment Insurance Act of 1911 had been introduced to keep the short term unemployed out of the workhouse.

After 1918 the poorest areas faced the highest claims on Poor Law rates. In 1921 the Labour Council of Poplar in East London controlled an area of high unemployment. The housing was poor and the rateable values were low. Hence the poor rate did not meet the demands for relief, and this was made worse by the fact that the Poor Law Guardians did not apply the Workhouse rule very strictly and they also paid out generous outdoor relief. In 1921 the authority fell into debt and refused to pay rates to the London County Council (LCC) for such services as the policing of London. Consequently 24 of their councillors were briefly imprisoned. They were released after giving an apology, but in a way victory was theirs because they continued to pay generous relief and, as unemployment fell, began to attract paupers from other boroughs.

The *Daily Express* criticized over generous boroughs. In August 1921 it described Islington:

Islington has found a substitute for the now unpopular dole.

The guardians have adopted a new scale of poor relief, by which many families will receive a larger weekly income than if the head of the household were fully employed.

A family composed of man and wife and six children, for example, will receive a total of £3 13s 6d weekly, made up by the addition to the following items:

Husband	12s 6d
Wife	12s 6d
6 children (5s for each child)	£1 10s 0d
Rent	15s 0d
1 cwt of coal	3s 6d
Total	£3 13s 6d

Poor Law administration cost the ratepayers of Islington £200,000 during the first six months of this year, as compared with £89,000 for a similar period in 1918.

(*Source: Daily Express*, 2 August 1921)

Do you think that this is a typical family? If not, why did the Daily Express *choose one with six children?*

No doubt the paper approved of the following action:

Jarrow Guardians have suspended the payment of poor relief to about twenty people who went for a motor coach trip costing five shillings each. The trippers have been ordered to appear before the relief committee.

(*Source:* Quoted in J. McMillan, *The Way it Was: 1914-1934*, Kimber, 1979)

What are the arguments for and against the action taken by the Islington and Jarrow Guardians?

Eventually Neville Chamberlain introduced the Local Government Act of 1929. He sought changes in the Poor Law, not for humanitarian reasons, but because he felt that the Boards of Guardians were inefficient and because of the inequality of the poor rates. So the Guardians were abolished and the county borough councils took over their duties, dealing with much larger areas. The local authorities established Public Assistance Committees to provide help for the poor.

ON REFLECTION:

In this chapter we have seen how the problems of the inter-war years led to change. Do you think the changes would have occurred without the large number of unemployed?

The Second World War and the Coming of the Welfare State

The First World War had seen the State become involved in the lives of the people. The Second World War was to see an even greater State involvement. The withdrawal of the British Army from Dunkirk by a multitude of small ships, and the bombing of London and many of the major cities, brought the people together as never before. The desire to defend the country and defeat Hitler provided the bond which brought all social classes together. By 1940 England was engaged in a "total war" in which both civilians and the Armed Forces were engaged. What is more, the various regulations by the State called for equal sacrifice. In this people's war, all were required to contribute either by enlisting or at home. Food shortages led to rationing, bombing led to evacuation and the various regulations applied equally, and did not distinguish between rich and poor.

The increased involvement by the State was in order that the war could be fought more effectively and scarce resources and manpower used as efficiently as possible. During the war, production in the factories and of food increased dramatically and there was a feeling that this could be continued into peacetime.

EVACUATION   When the bombing of the cities began, not only children but also whole schools were evacuated from the high risk areas.

My parents lived in a comfortable three bedroomed semi-detached house in Blackpool. I was the only child and therefore the spare bedroom was requisitioned – and one day in 1941, two girls, who were slightly older than me, were boarded on us. They came from a Manchester slum and I had to give up my larger bedroom, so that the two sisters could be together. Their language, dress and general habits came as quite a shock to me and I shall never forget my mother combing the lice from their hair into a tray. There were also shocks for the girls for they had never sat down to a meal before, and were unused to using cutlery, much preferring to pick the plate up.

(*Source:* A Blackpool resident, 7 years old in 1941)

Both families became aware of each other's lives. How important for future reform was this type of awareness?

Bombing, evacuation, the rehousing and care of homeless families involved the Government in dealing with welfare problems. The German bombers did not discriminate and both the slums and the suburbs of our cities and towns suffered. It was truly a people's war and the nation believed that at war's end there should be reform to ensure the future and prevent a return to the unemployment and hardships of the 1930s. By contrast, many in 1919 had hoped for a return to the pre-war days.

Children board a train for a safer destination. Evacuation meant that children were separated from their families, but protected from bombing raids.

We must indeed beware of defining these values in purely 19th century terms. If we speak of democracy we do not mean a democracy which maintains the right to vote but forgets the right to work and the right to live. If we speak of freedom we do not mean a rugged individualism which excludes social organisation and economic planning. If we speak of equality we do not mean a political equality nullified by social and economic privilege. If we speak of economic reconstruction we think less of maximum (though this job too will be required) than of equitable distribution . . . . The new order cannot be based on the preservation of privilege whether the privilege be that of a country, of a class or of an individual.

(*Source: The Times*, 1 July 1940)

Why does The Times *warn us against defining our values in purely nineteenth-century terms?*

The ideas for post-war reconstruction began long before victory was either assured or a possibility. In 1943 William Beveridge argued that when the peace came it must benefit the people.

[It] represents simply a refusal to take victory in war as an end in itself; it must be read as a determination to understand and to approve the end beyond victory for which sacrifices are being required.

(*Source:* William Beveridge, *The Pillars of Security*, 1943)

The Dunkirk spirit in the dark days of 1940 prepared the way for family welfare legislation. Reports as early as 1939 on the conditions of evacuated families (their physical conditions and various vitamin deficiencies) raised the conscience of the whole country.

THE EXPANDING STATE

Richard M. Titmuss described the way in which the State sought to make the best use of limited supplies and resources and took responsibility for those in need:

. . . the evacuation of mothers and children and the bombing of homes

---

during 1939-40 stimulated inquiry and proposals for reform long before victory was even thought possible. This was an important experience, for it meant that for five years of war the pressures for a higher standard of welfare and a deeper comprehension of social justice steadily gained in strength. And during this period, despite all the handicaps of limited resources in men and materials, a big expansion took place in the responsibilities accepted by the State for those in need.

(*Source:* R.M. Titmuss, "Problems of Social Policy", *History of the Second World War*, HMSO, 1950)

Look back to the earlier chapters to explain why these new ideas where radically different from laissez-faire and self help. Were these the values of the nineteenth century which The Times *wished to abandon?*

State Welfare benefits

a for children

i. school meals 1940 1 in 30 school children had school dinners

1945 1 in 3 school children had school dinners

cost free for the poor (14% of all children)

4½d (later 5d) for the rest

ii. school milk free for the poor, ½d for the rest

iii. free immunization against diphtheria, etc.

free issue of cod liver oil.

b for adults

1939 State nurseries for children of working mothers

Emergency Medical Service introduced – included ⅔ of all hospitals.

1940 Supplementary benefits for the old – to counter inflation.

1941 Family means test abolished.

(*Source:* various)

How far were these measures in line with the National Efficiency campaign of the early 1900s (see chapter 4) and how far did they go beyond it?

THE BEVERIDGE REPORT

In June 1941 Sir William Beveridge was appointed Chairman of an Inter-Departmental Committee to examine the existing range of social insurance and to make recommendations for the future. The Report was published in December 1942 and became one of the most influential of the twentieth century, selling 635,000 copies. Beveridge aimed to abolish "that poverty which is due to the interruption or loss of earning power" and believed that equal contributions by all should bring equal benefits. In this he was calling for the abolition of any form of means test. Need would be a sufficient reason for a claim, and he argued that there should be a minimum subsistence level in return for compulsory contributions.

Needs: The needs to be covered are of seven kinds, including as one the composite needs of a married woman.

C. Childhood, provided for by allowances till 14 or if in full-time education, till 16.

O. Old Age, including premature old age, met by pension beginning from 65 for man and 60 for a woman normally, but beginning earlier for proved permanent invalidity.

D. Disability, that is to say inability through illness or accident to pursue a gainful occupation, met by disability and invalidity benefits.

U. Unemployment, that is to say, inability to obtain paid employment by a person dependent on it and physically fit for it, met by unemployment benefit.

F. Funeral Expenses of self or any person for whom responsible, met by funeral grant.

L. Loss in Gainful Occupation other than Employment, e.g. bankruptcy, fire, theft, met by loss grant.

M. Marriage Needs of a Woman, including provision for:

1. Setting up of a home, met by furnishing grant.

2. Maternity met by maternity grant in all cases, and in the case of a married woman also gainfully employed by maternity benefit for a period before and after confinement.

3. Interruption of husband's earning, by his disability or unemployment, met by dependant benefit.

4. Widowhood, met by pension at various rates corresponding to needs and by credit of contributions for unemployment and disability.

5. Separation, i.e. end of husband's maintenance by desertion or legal separation, met by adaptation of widowhood provisions.

6. Old Age, met by pension at 60, with provision for antedating if husband's earning capacity is stopped by old age.

7. Incapacity for household duties, met by grant to meet expenses of paid help in illness.

8. Funeral Grant for self or any person for whom responsible after separation from husband.

(*Source:* W.H. Beveridge, Heads of a Scheme for Social Security, 11 December 1942)

To Beveridge the five things to be challenged and defeated were want, disease, ignorance, squalor and idleness. Which of these was the above extract aimed at? How far do you think it would be effective?

Beveridge saw his recommendations in line with the earlier gradual developments. He called it "a British Revolution".

The Report was welcomed by all parties within the Coalition. The Labour Party called for its immediate adoption, but Churchill, the wartime Prime Minister, felt that nothing must detract from the war effort. However, the consensus was there, and amongst the Conservative supporters of Beveridge were those who later were to be the leaders of their party.

FURTHER ACTION In 1943 and 1944 a series of White Papers were prepared.

(a) Educational Reconstruction, 1943

Introduction.

The Government's purpose in putting forward the reforms described in this Paper is to secure for children a happier childhood and a better start in life; to ensure a fuller measure of education and opportunity for young people and to provide means for all of developing the various talents with which they are endowed and so enriching the inheritance of the country whose citizens they are. The new educational opportunities must not, therefore, be of a single pattern. It is just as important to achieve diversity as it is to ensure equality of educational opportunity. But such diversity must not impair the social unity within the educational system which will open the way to a more closely knit society and give us strength to face the tasks ahead. The war has revealed afresh the resources and character of the British people – an enduring possession that will survive all the material losses inevitable in the present struggle. In the youth of the nation we have our greatest national asset. Even on a basis of mere expediency, we cannot afford not to develop this asset to the greatest advantage. It is the object of the present proposals to strengthen and inspire the younger generation. For it is as true to-day, as when it was first said, that 'the bulwarks of a city are its men'.

(*Source: White Paper on Educational Reconstruction*, HMSO, 1943, quoted in J.S. Maclure, *Educational Documents, England and Wales 1816-1967*, Chapman and Hall, 1967)

The report proposed a tripartite system of secondary education – Grammar, Technical and Modern, with the 11 + examination to determine which type of school children should attend. The report was largely adopted in the 1944 Education Act. Why do you think this report could only have been produced during a period of war? How was the system adopted in 1944 changed in the 1960s? The great benefit of the 1944 Act was that it extended compulsory and free education to 14.

(b) A National Health Service, 1944

This was organized by the new Minister for Reconstruction, Lord Woolton, and the White Paper met with agreement from all groups within the Coalition. It proposed much more than a hospital service and recommended "a comprehensive service covering every branch of medical and allied activity". Free treatment was to be provided out of taxation. However, the British Medical Association (BMA) opposed it:

[they] tried frantically to discredit it, finding sinister implications of bureaucratic control lurking everywhere under the idealistic promises of the White Paper . . . the B.M.A. kept up an unedifying racket until the very eve of the new service's creation.

(*Source:* A. Calder, *The People's War*, 1969)

What was the BMA's main fear?

These unemployed men are protesting against their poverty. They needed help from the State and did not get it.

(c) Employment Policy, 1944

This committed the Coalition members (Liberal, Labour and Conservative) to a policy of full employment which was to be achieved by a combination of public spending, public works and state controls. Beveridge also issued a report called *Full Employment in a Free Society*. Both reports owed much to the ideas of John Maynard Keynes, an economist, who believed that it was necessary for governments to spend in order to achieve full employment and to avoid depression. The fact that the idea that balancing the Budget was not always the first priority was significant in that it was accepted by all the Coalition parties.

(d) Social Insurance, 1944

This became the basis of the 1946 National Insurance Act.

THE 1945 ELECTION

Churchill believed that the Coalition should only continue as long as the war, and so after the surrender of Germany on 7 May 1945 he offered Clement Atlee, the Labour leader, the choice of an immediate election, or one after the defeat of Japan. Atlee plumped for an early election, and so Churchill resigned and called an election for 5 July 1945. The election issue became "freedom versus socialism" and Churchill lost votes by declaring that no socialist system can be established without a political police. "They would have to fall back on some form of Gestapo." In spite of this there was much consensus as to the future.

The Conservative Manifesto 1945

National well-being is founded on good employment, good housing and good health. But there always remain those personal hazards of fortune, such as illness, accident or loss of a job, or industrial injury, which may leave the individual and his family unexpectedly in distress. In addition, old age, death and child-birth throw heavy burdens upon the family income.

One of our most important tasks will be to pass into law and bring into action as soon as we can a nation-wide and compulsory scheme of National Insurance based on the plan announced by the Government of all Parties in 1944 . . . .

The health services of the country will be made available to all citizens. Everyone will contribute to the cost, and no one will be denied the attention, the treatment or the appliances he requires because he cannot afford them.

We propose to create a comprehensive health service covering the whole range of medical treatment from the general practitioner to the specialist, and from the hospital to convalescence and rehabilitation; and to introduce legislation for this purpose in the new Parliament.

The Labour Manifesto 1945

Housing will be one of the greatest and one of the earliest tests of a Government's real determination to put the nation first. Labour's pledge is firm and direct – it will proceed with a housing programme with the maximum practical speed until every family in this island has a good standard of accommodation . . . .

The best health services should be available for all . . . (through) the new National Health Service a . . . Labour government will press on rapidly with legislation extending social insurance over the necessary wide field to all.

Atlee's radio broadcast 5 June 1945

The men and women of this country who have endured great hardships in war are asking what kind of life awaits them in peace . . . they need good homes, sufficient food, clothing and the amenities of life, employment and leisure, and social provision for accident, sickness and old age. For their children they desire an educational system that will give them the chance to develop all their faculties.

Using the above extracts, list the points on which the two parties agreed. Do you think this shows that there was a general consensus (agreement) between the parties over welfare in 1945?

The Labour Party won 393 seats against the Conservatives' 213. Clearly the electorate had voted for reform. Many of the Labour ministers had gained experience in the wartime Coalition, and none of them had held office in the last Labour Government of 1929-31.

Whichever Party had been elected would have faced huge problems – the war against Japan was still continuing and huge debts had been built up during the war. Half the population was still in the War Services or in war industries and soon there was inflation and a financial crisis. Nevertheless the Labour Government up to 1951 sought to introduce the much needed social reforms.

One of the last Acts of the Coalition had been the Family Allowances Act of 1945 which gave an allowance for every child after the first. The amount was 5 shillings (25p) per child paid out of national taxation to every mother, regardless of income. Books of coupons were issued and they could be cashed at the Post Office. By 1949 4.7 million family allowances had been given.

REFORMS OF THE LABOUR GOVERNMENT

1946 The National Insurance Act

The Act implemented the recommendations of the 1944 White Paper and paid flat rate benefits of 26 shillings with a further 16 shillings for a wife and 7s 6d per child. This was higher than existing payments and contributions were now compulsory and at a flat rate. The payments were 4s 11d weekly with the Government and the employer also contributing.

The benefits comprised:

Unemployment Benefit	– paid after three days of unemployment, up to 180 days (not paid to the self-employed).
Sickness Benefit	– paid after three days when prevented from working through sickness. Could be paid in full up to retirement.
Retired Benefit	– Paid to men at 65 and women at 60, at a set rate.
Widows' Pensions	– Geared to the age of the widow, but widow had to have been married for 10 years.
Maternity Benefit	– A single payment to the mother on the birth of her baby. Working mothers received an allowance for 13 weeks after the birth.
Guardians Allowance	– Paid if one of the parents had been insured.
Funeral Allowance	– A lump sum to cover the cost of the funeral.

i. *How did this Act guard against interruption of earnings, extra expenditure and death of the breadwinner?*
ii. *How far did the Act fulfil the needs as outlined by Beveridge on p.47?*
iii. *Why do you think that some Labour MPs (such as Sydney Silverman and Barbara Castle) objected to parts of the Act? Did it fail to match socialist expectations?*

1948 The National Assistance Act

If the benefits under the National Insurance Act were insufficient, if one's contributions were insufficient, or had not been made one could apply for a supplementary allowance from the National Assistance Board (the old Assistance Board). The Act was important and though the claim was means tested, it provided a safety net outside the Poor Law. Poor Law legislation was finally repealed and Aneurin Bevan rightly declared "At last we have buried the Poor Law."

1948 The National Health Act

The Wartime Coalition had supported many of the ideas behind a National

This cartoon by Zec appeared in the Daily Mirror *in September 1945. Aneurin ('Ny) Bevan was the mastermind behind the nationalization of Health Services.*

'Just spots before the eyes.... Don't worry, we'll soon cure that!'' *The new Labour Government soon began to put its election promises into action. The nationalisation of Health Services, under Aneurin Bevan, was high on the list.* **(September 9, 1945)**

Health Service and Aneurin Bevan, the Labour Minister of Health, was keen that the earlier recommendations should be implemented as soon as possible. Less than half the population of 46 million were covered by the National Insurance scheme and the rest were dependent either on private schemes, charity or nothing. Thus falling ill was still the fear of many and doctors' fees were a burden. Furthermore, hospital provision varied according to area. In the wealthy suburbs provision was good and there were many doctors and hospitals. On the other hand in the areas of need where the people could afford less, provision was often poor.

The National Health Bill met with little opposition in Parliament and was passed in 1946. The Act established a universal medical service available to all regardless of whether one was rich or poor. In effect 3,000 hospitals were nationalized and put under the control of 20 regional hospital groups. Dentistry, nursing, infant child care, maternity and mental health were all included, and health centres were to be found in every area. The Act was to be put into effect on 5 July, 1948 and Bevan had two years to persuade the doctors to join the scheme. The main objections of the doctors' professional association, the BMA, was the fear of becoming paid employees of the State, and losing their independence – ability to charge fees, buy and sell their practices. Initially some 66% of the doctors were against the Act.

The Doctors' Argument

. . . the association regards the points at issue as we regard them, not bargaining points but signs of the doctor being a free man, free to practise his science and art in his patients' best interests . . . we must not yield on any of the points which collectively or individually spell the doctor's freedom.

(*Source:* Quoted in A. Lindsey, *Socialised Medicine in England and Wales*, University of North Carolina Press, 1967)

The battle was hard fought and Bevan only won by buying off the hospital consultants, as he said "by stuffing their mouths with gold". He did this by allowing them to work part-time in the health service and at the same time charge fees to their private patients and also use hospital beds in National Health service hospitals where they could supervise their private patients. Eventually in May 1948 the BMA accepted the scheme and consequently 18,000 doctors and 14,000 chemists joined. The *Daily Mirror* wrote:

THE DAY IS HERE

You always wanted fuller protection against misfortune. You wanted the state to accept larger responsibility for the individual citizen who served it faithfully.
YOU WANTED SOCIAL SECURITY. FROM THIS DAY HENCE, YOU HAVE IT.

(*Source: Daily Mirror*, 5 July 1948)

WOOLWORTHS

Woolworth's always had a counter displaying spectacles. I often saw adults trying them on. There were only two conditions to be filled. One, did they fit you? And secondly, did they improve your sight? For the majority of people those were the only glasses they had before the National Health Service.

(*Source:* the author's wartime recollection)

A SCOTTISH DOCTOR

Dr Alastair Clarke was a family doctor in Clydebank two years before the arrival of the NHS. "I used to charge 1/6d for a consultation," he said, "They laid the money on the desk as they came in. It was all rather embarrassing. I used to charge 2/6d to 7/6d for a visit, the highest rate for foremen or under-managers. We'd send out the bills, but about a quarter would be bad debts and some you simply didn't bill because you knew they couldn't pay.

People always managed to find the money to bring their children. But the mothers would go without. When the NHS came in, all that emerged. Within six months I had 30 or 40 women come in who had been suffering gynaecological problems, many of them for years – women with a complete prolapse of the uterus who'd been wearing nappies and towels to hide the problem."

(*Source: The Independent* 4 July 1988)

Try and find more about how your family managed before 1948, and their reactions to the introduction of the NHS.

Thus 5 July 1948 is regarded as the birth date of the Welfare State. The sick and the disabled, the elderly, widows and orphans, families and the unemployed were now all covered. From the start the National Insurance element contributed only a small proportion of the total cost. The rest came from national taxation.

By December 1948 21 million people had received medical treatment and Bevan was shuddering "to think of the ceaseless cascade of medicine which is pouring down British throats". Increasing cost was a factor from the start and it dominated political arguments throughout the early 1950s, as it does today. Interestingly the surveys carried out at that time showed that once inflation had been taken into account, the overall cost was falling, and as a percentage of the Gross National Product (GNP) spending had fallen.

Dr Webster, Head of the Wellcome Unit for the History of Medicine in Oxford, was recently interviewed

The argument that the NHS is a "bottomless pit" creating a permanent expenditure crisis "has always been more myth than reality . . . . The real problem of the NHS was the expectation that a comprehensive service would be created on a budget more suitable to an austerity service. As a result, expenditure was held down to an artifically low level . . . ." Before 1960 hardly any new hospitals were built, with capital spending being cut every time there was a public spending problem. As a result, revenue was wasted on old buildings and plant, which were more costly to run than modern replacements would have been – a problem which still exists.

(*Source:* quoted in *The Independent*, 1988)

Various solutions have been tried to reduce costs. In 1951 the Labour Government introduced prescription charges and Aneurin Bevan resigned on principle. Since then charges on dental and optical work have been levied. Similarly, national insurance charges have been increased and are now set at various rates according to income. In the last decade three factors have added to the cost of the service:

a. the increasing age of the population,
b. the development in medicine which has led to such things as heart by-pass surgery and kidney dialysis machines which have either saved lives or kept people alive longer. However, they are extremely expensive.
c. as the numbers in hospital and in need of care rose, so the wage bill increases. Recently the nurses have had a wage increase, of which everyone approves, but this places strains on the budget.

SOCIAL SECURITY The other issue which has been increasingly discussed in the 1980s is social security spending – the money which goes to various groups in need. Diagram A illustrates how the money is distributed and Diagram B looks at it as a slice of the total government expenditure in 1988.

(Diagrams A and B – see page 55)

(*Source: Public Expenditure White Paper*, 1988)

What percentage of money goes towards what we would call the Welfare State?

Social security payments, especially unemployment, are a highly emotive

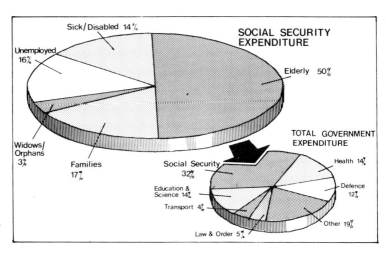

SOCIAL SECURITY
EXPENDITURE

Sick/Disabled 14%

Unemployed 16%

Elderly 50%

Widows/Orphans 3%

Families 17%

TOTAL GOVERNMENT
EXPENDITURE

Social Security 32%

Education & Science 14%

Transport 4%

Law & Order 5%

Health 14%

Defence 12%

Other 19%

Social security expenditure 1988.

issue. Look at pamphlets produced by the Department of Health and Social Security (DHSS) and try and work out who can claim and the amount. Many of the arguments for tighter controls, or even reduced benefits, may seem similar to those used in the nineteenth century. Self help or support? Circumstances change, however, for in the twentieth century the State plays a much greater role and it would be difficult to go back to truly "Victorian Values", although aspects of the Victorian system may be modified and updated.

ON REFLECTION:

Historians differ as to how precisely the Welfare State of 1948 came into existence. The two main alternative arguments are these:

"The decisive event in the evolution of the Welfare State was the Second World War."

"The Welfare State was essentially the culmination of half a century of piecemeal social reform now carried to its logical conclusion."

Look back through this book and find evidence which supports each idea. Then try and write your own conclusion.

The other aspect which many find puzzling is that in spite of all the effort, legislation and money which has been spent on the Welfare State, the poor still exist, and the need is still great. Photographs of people sleeping rough under the arches at Charing Cross, stories of the old dying of hypothermia at Christmas are tragedies which are repeated each year. Adequate housing, sufficient jobs and care for the elderly are all examples which everyone would wish to see, but one factor that changes with time is our definition of poverty.

Poverty: a definition

. . . people must have an income which enables them to take part in the life of the community. They must be able to keep themselves reasonably fed, and well enough dressed to keep their self-respect and to attend interviews for jobs. Their homes must be reasonably warm; their children should not feel shamed by the quality of their clothing; the family must be able to visit relatives . . . read newspapers . . . retain their membership of trade unions and churches. And they must be able to live in a way which ensures that public officials, doctors, teachers, landlords and others treat them with the courtesy due to every member of the community.

(*Source:* Supplementary Benefits Commission Definition of Poverty, 1938)

Do you think the definition of poverty would be the same today? If not how would you define it? How would Edwin Chadwick and the supporters of the New Poor Law have defined poverty in the 1830s?

It may even be worth asking how far our definition of the Welfare State, and the areas in which the State should help the individual have changed since 1948. 40 years ago it was envisaged as a universal service available to all. Present day political arguments revolve around the degree to which this should be modified or supported. It is a vital question for every citizen, and one on which everyone should have a point of view. Hopefully this book will have given you the evidence from which to reach a conclusion, and also the understanding that issues are often complex and that they often depend upon one's understanding and interpretation of the past.

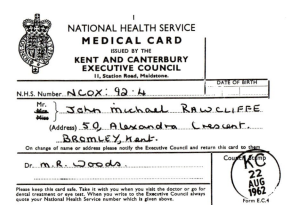

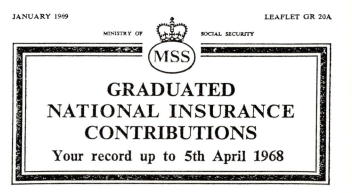

Various leaflets and cards. Try to find similar examples from your family. Note that in 1969 the Department of Social Services was separate, then linked with Health and in July 1988 was separated again.

Glossary

able-bodied	after 1834 the able-bodied, who were without work could only obtain relief (help) inside the Workhouse
Allowance system	the general name for the system of giving help to the poor before 1834
artisan	a mechanic, usually a skilled manual worker
Bolshevik revolution	the successful Communist Revolution led by Lenin in Russia in November 1917
bye-law	a local law passed by a local authority
cholera	an infectious and deadly disease which was at its peak in 1831, 1848-9, 1854, and 1856. At first it was believed that it was spread in the air by smell, but later it was discovered to be spread by sewage-polluted water
coalition	the joining together of 2 or more political parties to govern in an emergency, e.g. in wartime, during the Great Depression
collectivism	the belief that the State should take responsibility and aid the people
consensus	general agreement when sufficient beliefs are held in common
conscription	a system by which all fit men between certain ages must join the armed forces in time of war
DHSS	Department of Health and Social Security
depression	or slump, when too many goods are being produced and unemployment increases
dole	the payment made to the unemployed
dreadnought	an iron-clad battleship, named after the first, HMS *Dreadnought*
Evangelical	a Christian who believes that he should take his faith to the people
Fabian socialist	a socialist who believes that reforms and change should evolve by peaceful, gradual means
GNP	Gross National Product – the total wealth of the country
humanitarianism	the belief that one should help those in need
hypothermia	a dangerous condition caused by extreme cold, from which babies and old people may die
laissez-faire	the belief that the Government should not interfere in the life of the individual
Means test	the test to determine whether one should receive help
nationalization	the process whereby the State takes over and controls certain industries
Overseer of the Poor	one of the appointed Poor Law Officials
pauper	poor, usually living on Poor Relief or charity
penury	when one has no money to live on
philanthropy	charity in the form of money or active help
Poor Law Union	a group of parishes formed together after 1834 to supervise the poor in their area
poor rate	money collected from all householders to provide for the poor
poor relief	aid or relief given to the poor. From the sixteenth century parishes were obliged to aid their poor
privation	being deprived, e.g. of food, shelter, etc.
rateable value	the amount a property is assessed for rates
requisition	to take over
Salvation Army	Christian organization formed by William Booth in 1879, giving charity to the poor and needy
secular	not religious; relating to the present world
self-help	the belief that one should seek to help and improve oneself without support from others

Shaftesbury Society	founded to support the ideas of Lord Ashley, later the Earl of Shaftesbury, the great Victorian social reformer
slump	an industrial depression, where goods outweigh demand and unemployment is high
slum	an area of poor, overcrowded housing
Social Services	the agencies which cope with, and give help to the individual when in need
Temperance	the belief that alcohol causes problems. The Temperance movement advocated abstinence and urged their supporters to sign the Pledge, and not to drink
unadulterated food	food which is not a danger to health
utilitarian	the idea developed by Jeremy Bentham (1748–1832) that one should test everything by its usefulness and efficiency rather than by tradition
vaccination	an innoculation against disease. At first a cow vaccine was used against smallpox
vagrant	one who has no settled home who wanders from place to place
Whigs	one of the two main political parties along with the Tories
Workhouse test	In 1834 the conditions in the workhouse were made very severe in order to deter the able bodied and force him to take work
YMCA	Young Men's Christian Association

Sources

a review of the types of evidence and sources used in this book

Diaries	Early working-class diaries are few, but local record offices often contain ones which have been deposited by local people, and several of the well known ones have been published, e.g. *The Crossman Diaries*, in which Richard Crossman gave details of his work in politics.
Directories	Commercial directories are available for virtually every town, and certainly for every county. *Whites* and *Kelly's* are the most famous. They will enable you to build up a picture of your local community, through the official lists of householders and commercial firms, societies, groups, Boards of Guardians, etc. They also include a range of excellent advertisements, e.g. for local hospitals seeking voluntary contributions.
Poor Law Material	These are the working documents of the Parish, and later the Board of Guardians. Overseers' accounts, workhouse dietaries, minutes of the Board of Guardians are examples of what you will find.
Official Literature	In the last two centuries a wide range of official publications have been produced ranging from Royal Commission enquiries into the Poor Law (1905-9) to the White Papers such as those on Insurance (1944) and Health (1944)
Newspapers	The Press is an excellent source. Some papers such as *The Times* publish an index, but you could dip into known months and years when something important occurred, e.g. July 1948, National Health Service. Reference libraries often take *KEESINGS Archives* which is a weekly report of domestic and international events. It has a running index which is very useful.
Cartoons	These can give insights into the mood and attitudes of the time. Look at the weekly magazine *Punch* and various cartoonists, e.g. Low in the *Daily Mail*. However, as with newspapers you need to be aware of their political bias.
Oral evidence	In a subject such as this the Welfare State, where the topic is an ongoing one, evidence can still be collected, e.g. the DHSS was divided into two sections in July 1988 so you will be a source for the future. Equally your parents and grandparents will have much to say on the Second World War, the development of the National Health Service since 1948, prescription charges, etc. However, you need to be able to check what is said against the actual details of what happens. Their *opinion* will be invaluable.

Local histories	These are very useful for building up a picture of your area in the nineteenth and twentieth centuries. They are unlikely to have specific chapters on the Welfare State, but will contain details of how, for example, the Union Workhouse may have become a hospital and now belongs to the Area Health Authority.
Literature	Novels, poetry and other literature can give us important insights into life in a particular time. Dickens wrote vividly on the urban poor in the nineteenth century and there are many books on the Great Depression. However literature is not history and is not intended to be such, so beware.
Photographs	Photographic evidence is invaluable and often available in postcard form. You could then compare photographs of a hospital taken, say, 60 years ago, with ones taken today.

Book List

There are very few books written specifically on the Welfare State. Of these at the school level are S. Wood, *The British Welfare State (1900-50)* (CUP, 1982), and R.C. Birch, *The Shaping of the Welfare State* (Longman, 1976), part of the A Level Seminar Studies series. A useful document pack is also produced by Longman, *The Beginning of the Welfare State*. For adults, D. Fraser's *The Evolution of the British Welfare State* (Macmillan, 1973) is excellent.

Otherwise it is best to use books on specific aspects such as the Poor Law or Public Health where there is a range of books such as R. Waters, *Edwin Chadwick, the Poor Law and Public Health* (Longman *Then and There* series, 1969) and M.A. Crowther, *The Workhouse System 1834-1929* (Methuen, 1983).

There are biographies of all the major political personalities such as Winston Churchill, Lloyd George, Edwin Chadwick and Aneurin Bevan, and the Encyclopaedia Britannica entries are often a good starting point. There are now also several excellent anthologies of documents with good introductions. Notable ones are those written by E. Royston Pike such as *Human Documents of the Age of the Forsytes* (the 1880s and 1890s), Allen and Unwin, 1969, and *Human Documents of the Lloyd George Era* (1972), and D. Read, *Documents of Edwardian England*, (Harrap, 1973).

For GCSE there are several excellent general text books such as S.R. Gibbons, *Britain 1945-85* (Blackie, 1986), J. Wilkes, *The United Kingdom: a social and economic history* (CUP 1984) and J. Robotham, *Social and Economic History of Britain* (Longman, 1986).

Money

Always consider what money and wages could buy rather than what might appear low prices. A doctor's bill of 2/6d would be beyond the man earning only £1 a week.

240d = 100p = £1

sixpence ("a tanner")	6d	2½p
shilling	1/-	5p
florin	2/-	10p
half crown	2/6d	12½p
ten shillings ("10 bob")	10/-	50p
a pound	20/-	£1

Timeline

PERIOD	DATES	EVENTS
The Hanoverians **1714–1837**	1722/3	Workhouse Act.
	c. 1760	Agricultural Revolution.
	1781/2	Gilbert's Workhouse Act.
	c. 1780–1830	Industrial Revolution.
	1793–1815	Revolutionary and Napoleonic Wars against France.
	1802	Health and Morals of Apprentices Act.
	1815	End of the Napoleonic Wars.
	1831	First Cholera outbreak.
	1832	Royal Commission on the Poor Law.
	1833	State grant to Education.
		Factory Act.
	1834	Poor Law Amendment Act.
The Victorians **1837–1901**	1837	Civil Registration of Births and Deaths.
	1842	Mines Act.
		Report on The Sanitary Conditions of the Labouring Population.
	1847	Ten Hour Act.
	1848	Public Health Act.
	1866	Sanitary Act.
	1872	Public Health Act.
	1875	Artisans Dwelling Act.
	1888	Local Government Act.
	1899–1902	Second Boer War.
Edwardians **1901–1910**	1906	Liberal Victory over Conservatives.
	1908	Old Age Pensions, Labour Exchanges established. Children Act.
	1909	Lloyd George's Budget.

Timeline Notes: c: (circa) around about that time

SIGNIFICANCE	OTHER IMPORTANT EVENTS
Parishes with consent of majority of inhabitants allowed to purchase or hire buildings for lodging, keeping, maintaining and employing the poor. Those refusing to enter lost all right to relief. Small parishes allowed to combine for this purpose.	
More commercial approach to farming enclosures, crop rotation. Provides food for growing towns.	
Named after the MP for Lichfield. Parishes allowed to combine and employ paid guardians of the poor and JPs would supervise the new system. The institutions were still poorhouses rather than workhouses.	
Beginning of the Factory system and growth of towns. Public health problems increased.	
Many families split. Pressures on the Poor Law provisions.	**1801** First national census, from then on, held every 10 years (except in 1941).
First Government involvement in hours and conditions of children, but ineffective because no means of enforcement.	
Flooding of labour market by returning troops.	
Formation of Central Board of Health.	**1829** Metropolitan Police Act.
Brought about by rising costs. Work of Edwin Chadwick and influence of utilitarian ideas.	**1832** First Reform Act; first reform of Parliament.
Made to the voluntary societies. Amount small, but the first State grant.	**1833** Emancipation of slavery.
Introduced supervision by four inspectors. Precedent for future.	
Formation of Poor Law Unions and workhouse test. Triumph of utilitarian ideas.	**1835** Municipal Corporations Act: towns with charters could now elect a mayor and council and levy rates.
Enabled accurate statistics to be kept.	
Breach of laissez-faire: women and children could no longer work underground.	**1840** Free vaccination.
Work of Chadwick. Brought public health problems to a wider public.	
Victory for 10 Hour Movement, reducing hours in the factories.	**1847** Liverpool the first town to appoint a Medical Officer of Health.
After another cholera outbreak Boards of Health could be established.	**1849** Dr John Snow links cholera with poor water.
To give powers to towns public health.	**1875** Work of Joseph Chamberlain in Birmingham: redevelopment and slum clearance and taking over of private water and gas companies.
Brought together best of previous legislation.	
Local authorities allowed to raise rates to demolish slum housing.	
Boroughs and County Boroughs established.	**1890** Charles Booth: *In Darkest England*.
Sets back Chamberlain's ideas on pensions because of cost.	**1902** Education Act: Secondary education introduced.
With a large majority able to introduce social reforms.	**1909-**
Pensions as of right. Payable at the Post Office.	**1911** Crisis leads to Parliament Act and reduction of the powers of the House of Lords.
Rejected by House of Lords.	

Timeline

PERIOD	DATES	EVENTS
	1909	Poor Law Reports.
	1911	National Insurance Act.
	1914-1918	First World War.
	1916	Lloyd George Prime Minister of the Coalition.
Inter-War 1919–1939	1918	Fisher's Education Act.
	1919	Addison's Housing Act. Establishment of the Ministry of Health.
	1920	Unemployment Insurance Act.
	1923	Chamberlain's Housing Act.
	1924	Wheatley's Housing Act.
	1929	Local Government Act.
	1931	Fall of Labour Party.
		Dole cut.
	1935	Unemployment Assistance Board.
	1939	Outbreak of Second World War.
Second World War 1939–45	1940	National Milk Scheme.
	1942	Beveridge Report.
	1944	Education Act.
Post-War World	1945	Election.
	1945	Family Allowance Act.
	1946	National Insurance Act.
	1946	National Health Act.
	1947	Town and Country Planning Act.
	1948	Introduction of the National Health Service.
	1948	National Assistance Act.
	1948	Children's Act.
	1951	Prescription charges.
	1965	Labour Government issued Circular Oct. 65.
	1968	Departments of Health and Social Security joined.
	1971	Family Income Supplement.
	1988	Social Credit introduced.
	1988	DHSS split again into two separate Ministries.
	1988	New Education Act.

Timeline Notes: c: (circa) around about that time

SIGNIFICANCE	OTHER IMPORTANT EVENTS
Majority and minority reports reveal gulf of feeling. Health and Unemployment insurance introduced for first time by the State. First total war: increasing involvement by the State. Succeeds Asquith. Great wartime Prime Minister.	**1917** Bolshevik Revolution in Russia.
School compulsory to age of 14. Sees introduction of council housing (Homes for Heroes). Widens Act of 1911. The Conservative answer to housing: more subsidies to private builders. Labour's brief minority government (1924). Work of Chamberlain. End of many aspects of the Poor Law. National Government under Labour leader, Ramsay Macdonald. Means test introduced. Emergency Medical Service introduced.	**1919** Treaty of Versailles: end of war with Germany. **1926** General Strike. **1929** Wall Street Crash in USA: collapse of Stock Market. . . **1930** Leads to Great Depression in Europe.
For postwar reconstruction. "Secondary Education for all".	**1940** Churchill Coalition Prime Minister.
Labour victory. Atlee Prime Minister. Established a universal child allowance of 5 shillings for the second and subsequent children. Financed by the Government. A new social insurance scheme, covering the whole population from "the cradle to the grave". Work of Aneurin Bevan. Gave more power to local authorities to plan their housing. National Assistance Board gives extra money (Supplementary Benefit, 1966) to those in need who could not work. Local Authorities to set up Children's Departments. Growing costs led the Labour Government to introduce charges. Local authorities told to draw up plans for comprehensive education. DHSS now under one Cabinet Minister. New method of calculation for payment of benefit. Argued that it was too large to keep as one Department. First major Education Act since 1944. National Curriculum and testing introduced.	**1945** End of War with Germany. **1945** End of War with Japan. **1953/4** Food rationing ended. **1965** Child Poverty Action Group founded. **1979** Conservative Government elected under Mrs Thatcher.

Index

00004148

How Much Should Immigration Be Restricted?

Andrew Langley

First published in Great Britain by Heinemann Library, Halley Court, Jordan Hill, Oxford OX2 8EJ, part of Harcourt Education.

Heinemann is a registered trademark of Harcourt Education Ltd.

Editorial: Andrew Farrow and Rebecca Vickers
Design: Steve Mead and Q2A Solutions
Picture Research: Melissa Allison
Production: Alison Parsons
Originated by Chroma Graphics Pte. Ltd.
Printed and bound in China by Leo Paper Group

ISBN 978 0 431 11008 0
12 11 10 09 08
10 9 8 7 6 5 4 3 2 1

British Library Cataloguing in Publication Data
Langley, Andrew
How much should immigration be restricted? –
(What do you think?)
1. Emigration and immigration – Government policy – Juvenile literature 2. Emigration and immigration – Juvenile literature
I. Title
325.1

ISBN-13: 9780431110080

Acknowledgements
The publishers would like to thank the following for permission to reproduce photographs:
©Corbis pp. **29** (epa/Scanpix/Wilhelmsen_Group/Ho-Tampa), **15** (Howard Davies), **26** (Mimi Mollica), **35** (Photo by J. Emilio Flores For The New York Times), **14** (Reuters), **25** (Reuters/Carlos Barria), **47** (Reuters/Mathieu Belanger); ©Empics p. **39** (PA Photos/PA Archive); ©Getty Images pp. **40**, **8** (AFP Photo/Denis Sinyakov), **23** (AFP Photo/Mandel Ngan), p. **45** (Gary Williams), **42** (Joe Raedle); Library of Congress/George Grantham Bain Collection p. **10**; Courtesy of Middle School Public Debate Program p. **48**; ©2006, Nick Anderson. Distributed by The Washington Post Writers Group. Reprinted with Permission p. **50**; ©PA Photos pp. **33**, **21** (AP Photo/Gregory Bull), **18** (AP Photo/Jack Kurtz, Pool), **4** (AP Photo/Matt York), **30** (AP Photo/Rob Griffith); ©Photoedit, Inc. p. **7** (Myrleen Ferguson Cate); ©UPPA pp. **13** (Photoshot), **36** (Photoshot/Mark Thomas).

Cover photo of border fence reproduced with permission of ©Corbis/Sygma/JP Laffont. Wire frame photo from ©istockphoto.com/angelhell.

Every effort has been made to contact copyright holders of any material reproduced in this book. Any omissions will be rectified in subsequent printings if notice is given to the publishers.

The publishers would like to thank Mary Kelly for her assistance with the preparation of this book.

Table of Contents

Some words are printed in bold, **like this**. You can find out what they mean in the Glossary on pages 54–55.

> *Illegal entry*

A man climbs over a fence at the international border at Nogales, between the United States and Mexico. There are plenty of clues in the picture to show which side is which.

How Much Should Immigration Be Restricted?

Since human history began, people have been on the move. They have travelled in search of food, water, jobs, or wealth. Some have gone short distances—to the next village or town. Others have gone much further—to a different country or even a different continent.

All of these travellers were **migrants**. They migrated to settle in another place. What is the difference between a migrant and an **immigrant**? If a migrant moves *into* your country or region, he or she is an *immigrant*. Someone who migrates *out* of your country is called an **emigrant**.

People have been arguing about immigrants for hundreds of years. Sometimes they have blamed the newcomers for causing all kinds of problems, from overcrowding to lack of job opportunities. But at other times they have encouraged immigration, because of the economic benefits. The United States, for example, would not have grown into a great nation without the contribution of immigrants.

How much should immigration be restricted? It is a crucial debate in almost every nation in the world, and will have a key role in shaping the future of society. This book will help you to join in that debate.

How do you know what to think?

This series of books is called *What Do You Think*? The most important words in this question are the last two – *you* and *think*. First of all, *you* are the person being asked the question. You are involved, and what matters is your answer to the question. Secondly, you are being asked to *think*. Your opinion matters, but this does not just mean copying what someone else says. It's your opinion that counts.

Is there a "right" answer?

Suppose somebody asks you "What is two plus two?" This is a simple question, with just one correct answer: four. If you said "three" or "five" you would be wrong. This is a matter of fact, not opinion.

The title of this book asks a different kind of question: "How much should immigration be restricted?" This is not a simple question, and it does not have one correct answer. You cannot state definitely and finally that immigration is a good or a bad thing. However, you can have an opinion about it.

Everybody has opinions, about all kinds of topics. Sometimes they have strong opinions. Immigration is a subject that many people feel very strongly about. It can even make them angry, because they believe that they are right and others are wrong. In extreme cases, this leads to violence and hatred.

How do you form an opinion?

Do you think anger helps people to reach a sensible view on a topic? Does it make their arguments stronger? Or does it get in the way? It is far better to look at a subject calmly, and start out with an open mind. You will be surprised at what you may discover in this way.

You need a lot more than strong feelings if you want to form a worthwhile opinion. The first lesson is to think in a balanced way, so that you can look at all sides of a question before coming to a conclusion. You need to learn how to look for evidence, and how to study it. You must also be able to give good reasons for what you believe when you are discussing the subject with others.

The aim of this book is to help you think for yourself and make your own decisions about whether immigration should be controlled. To do this successfully, you need a clear set of steps that will lead you to a balanced and well-informed point of view.

> *What do you think?*

In debates or discussions with other students, family or friends, you must be able to back up your opinions with evidence and good reasoning. If you don't your argument will be weak and unsupported.

 Fact or feeling?

An **opinion** is a statement of what someone believes or feels or judges to be right. It is not a fact, but it can make use of facts.

Reasoning is the process of thinking, understanding, and forming opinions. This must be done logically, considering all possible options.

Evidence is the information (usually facts) we may use to form an opinion.

A **fact** is a statement that we can prove to be true.

> *Keep out!*

Members of a youth movement in Moscow, the capital of Russia, protest against illegal immigrants from countries which were once part of the Soviet Union.

Where's the evidence?

Anyone can have an opinion. You could make a judgement about a subject in a few seconds—just because that is what you feel at the time. But how long will it last? What's the use of having an opinion that does not stand up in a proper argument? A worthwhile and long-lasting opinion has to be based on evidence. Facts and other evidence give you a firm foundation to build your thinking on.

Where will you find this evidence? Look out for news stories in the papers or on radio and television. Visit your local library and look for books and magazines on the topic. The Internet will contain more facts, figures, case studies, and personal accounts on weblogs (blogs). Search for surveys, opinion polls, government reports, and anything else that gives useful information. Be careful to check these sources, and be aware of any **bias**.

Finally, don't forget that your own experiences could also be valuable. Are you part of a newly immigrant family? Do you live near one? Is one of your classmates a new arrival in your country? Talk to people around you and listen to the stories they may have to tell.

Listen to both sides of the argument

Don't start out with a set opinion in your head and then try to justify it. People on both sides of the argument will have something valuable to say. Keep an open mind and listen carefully to their views, even if you strongly disagree with them. When examining evidence, look out for a few sources that disagree with your views. You will learn a lot from them.

How much should immigration be restricted? Remember that this kind of question has no definite answer. It is a topic for debate and discussion. All the same, some people believe that an argument is not won by the person who is right, but by the person who is best at arguing.

Learn to be a critical thinker

These are the most important steps of all. By thinking critically, you will be able to use your evidence in the most powerful way. First, learn to ask your own questions about the evidence you find. Is it fact, or is it just somebody's idea? Is it honest, or is it biased to one side or the other? Who produced the evidence? Have they got an interest in trying to change your views?

Secondly, organize your findings. A jumble of facts and figures will only muddle you, so try to build them into a logical argument (think of it as a story, if you like). Have you got similar pieces of evidence that can be put together? Can you place facts side by side so that you can compare and contrast them? What is the best way to make your argument develop from one point to the next?

 Ask yourself ...

Have you formed an opinion?
No? Then ask yourself:
- ✔ What more information do you need to form an opinion?
- ✔ Where would you find that information?

Yes? Then ask yourself:
- ✔ How did you come to form that opinion?
- ✔ On what information did you base your opinion?
- ✔ What was the biggest factor in your decision?
- ✔ Have you ever changed your opinion?

> *Ellis Island, USA*

Between 1892 and 1954, over 12 million immigrants arrived at this island in New York Harbor from all over the world.

What Is An Immigrant?

Are you an immigrant? It's more than likely. Just about everybody in the world today is descended from someone who once moved from one region to another. Scientists believe that human life first developed in central Africa at least 5 million years ago. So, in theory, we could all call ourselves Africans.

From Africa, our ancestors gradually moved out into the rest of the world. They migrated to most parts of Europe and Asia. About 50,000 years ago, humans reached Australia. Much later, the first people crossed into North America and began migrating southwards. Very slowly, the world was filling up—with immigrants.

Today, more people are on the move than ever before. There are many reasons for this, from fast transport systems to the growing misery caused by long-running wars. Immigrants are not just looking for jobs, but also for safety from **oppression**, danger, poverty, and disease.

Many governments now see mass immigration as a big headache, and a threat to their countries' prosperity and security. Most have passed laws making it harder for foreigners to cross their borders and become permanent settlers. But is this going to solve the problem? There are now more than six billion humans spread across the world, and the total is rising by an extra million every week. Can a better solution be found?

Mixing and migrating

Where do you live? Where do you come from? These are two very different questions. You may live in the country where you were born. But where were your parents born? Go right back into your family history and you are almost certain to find that some of your roots are in another country.

Ask your classmates if they know their family history. What is their true racial background? It will almost certainly be much more complicated than they think.

Scientists are now using genetics to work out how human beings spread across the world:

The Biggest Family Tree Ever

Ever wondered where your family's ancestors roamed 60,000 years ago?

Now you can find out by participating in the world's most ambitious project tracing the **genetic** and migratory history of the human race.

Members of the general public from all over the world can supply their **DNA** to the Genographic Project, and scientists at The University of Arizona in Tucson will do the genetic analysis. The public DNA sampling is part of a larger undertaking to unravel the origins and migratory history of mankind thousands of years back in time by analyzing genetic samples from at least 200,000 people all over the world.

The project will reveal how our ancestors diversified into different groups and what routes they took as they spread out over the Earth.

[*Medical News Today* 16 Apr 2005, www.medicalnewstoday.com]

Who came from where?

These nations have been shaped by the endless series of migrations that have criss-crossed the world throughout our history.

The United States

In the past 500 years an amazing variety of immigrants has arrived in the United States to join the original Native Americans. Settlers from Europe brought in a **workforce** of slaves, forcibly moving at least ten million Africans to the Americas. After them came vast hordes of people in search of a better life. Most people came from Europe, especially Germany, Great Britain, Ireland,

Italy, Scandinavia, and Russia. Today, the United States is the top destination for people fleeing poverty in Mexico and Central America.

Latin America

After European soldiers conquered most of this huge area in the 1500s, large numbers of Spanish and Portuguese settlers moved in. They searched for mineral wealth and started cattle farms and sugar plantations. During the 1600s, other European settlers established colonies on Caribbean islands.

The United Kingdom

Celts, Romans, Vikings, Anglo-Saxons, and Normans were all immigrants who invaded Britain by 1066 and produced a rich mix of racial backgrounds. Since then, settlers from many more nations have arrived. In the last 50 years, the British population has been joined by large numbers of people from Commonwealth countries (such as Pakistan, India, Uganda, and Jamaica) and from Eastern Europe.

Australia

The aboriginal peoples lived alone here for at least 45,000 years. Then in 1788 the British founded a colony, which grew rapidly after the discovery of gold. After World War Two the Australian government encouraged millions of immigrants from all over Europe to move to Australia.

> *Flying the flag*

Two sisters from London wave Australian flags as they arrive in Sydney Harbour on an immigrant ship in 1949.

Why do people want to migrate?

Throughout history, migration has been an unstoppable force. People want to move, and sometimes nothing can hold them back. What makes them so determined? What are the factors which drive them to travel from one region to another, in spite of the possible danger and hostility?

The push factors

Several things can "push" people out of their own countries. The most powerful of these is fear. War causes death and destruction, and refugees migrate in search of shelter and safety. Since the 1980s, for example, many people have fled from Afghanistan because of invasion, civil war, and cruel government. Others leave their native lands because they are being persecuted for their religious beliefs or their ethnic background.

Poverty is another big "push" factor. Many countries are poor because of a harsh climate, or because of natural disasters, such as earthquakes and floods. These can cause famine, drought, diseases, and other hardships. Employment in poor countries is often hard to find or is badly paid.

The pull factors

There are positive attractions that "pull" migrants towards another country. Many of them are simply opposites of the "push" factors. Refugees from war and **persecution** look for countries that are peaceful and safe. People escaping from poverty go to countries where there are plenty of jobs that are better paid. Many of these immigrants send money from their wages to support their families back home.

Other "pull" factors are less obvious. Students become short-term immigrants in other countries because they have better schools or universities. People from wealthy countries often move to poorer ones that have better climates or lifestyles. People who have committed a serious crime in their own country sometimes run away to another where they know they will be safe from the police.

> *Modern-day Jewish exodus*

During the chaotic and confusing period of the break up of the former Soviet Union in 1990, many Jews feared persecution and fled to Israel.

What would make you want to swap countries?

Most people naturally love the country where they were born, and would hate to leave it. Many are also fearful of moving to a foreign land far away where they might be strangers with no friends and no jobs. But sometimes they have little choice.

> *Shelter from bloodshed*
>
> **Refugees from the 1999 civil war in the Serbian province of Kosovo find food and safety at a Red Cross camp in nearby Macedonia.**

Are you proud of your country and your nationality? Can you think of anything which would drive you to leave your friends and family and live somewhere else? Make a list of all the things that would be different. At the top of the list may be the language. Can you speak or understand any foreign languages? Then there is the daily life: every society has its own customs and ways of doing things, from eating and drinking to shopping and behaving in public. Would you be brave enough to face these difficulties?

Masses on the move

Migration throughout the world has increased hugely in the past two centuries. The peak period of mass movement lasted from the 1840s to the 1950s. Why did this happen? The **Industrial Revolution** was changing society and populations were growing fast, especially in Europe. More land and more jobs were desperately needed. There were big, "empty" countries waiting to be filled, and vast numbers of people wanting to move.

So the rush began. By the 1930s, over 60 million immigrants had moved to a new land. About half of these had arrived in the United States from all over the world. The rate has slowed since then, but large numbers of newcomers are still admitted to the United States each year. In the same period, Australia's population has rocketed from a few thousand to more than 20 million—largely thanks to immigration.

How many immigrants are there?

In 2005:
✔ 3 million immigrants became official long-term residents in a different country from where they were born
✔ Altogether, more than 190 million people moved to a different country (most of them for a short term, or illegally)
✔ 190 million people is equal to nearly 3 percent of the world's population
✔ This means that 97 percent of the world's population stayed at home.

Speeding up

How did these immigrants reach their goals? Most travelled before the age of aircraft and petrol engines. They crossed the oceans crammed in sailing ships or steamships. The voyages were often long, dangerous, and uncomfortable, with many migrants having to sleep out on deck. The journey from Europe to Australia took many weeks. Today, a jet aircraft can cover the same distance in less than 24 hours. Add to this the vast modern network of roads and rail tracks that cross entire continents, and fleets of safer and faster ships on the oceans, and you can see that travel today is much easier and more comfortable than ever before.

So, has immigration become easier?

The answer is yes and no. Yes, because of the better transport systems described above. No, because many countries now make it a lot more difficult for immigrants to gain legal access. In the last 100 years the world has become a much more definite place. Countries have formed themselves into what are called nation states, with their own special laws and cultural identities. They have clear borders, which are guarded and patrolled, and can only be crossed if you have the right kind of passport.

The gap between the rich and the poor

With such a large gap between the rich and poor countries, it is not surprising that migrants from poor countries want to leave their home lands. This chart gives you information about some of the richest and poorest countries in the world. GDP means annual gross domestic product. It is the amount of money a country earns in a year from all of its goods and services. If you divide GDP by the number of people in the population, you can get some idea of the annual income of individuals.

Country	GDP per inhabitant in US$
Luxembourg	$68,800
United Arab Emirates	$49,700
United States	$43,500
Canada	$35,200
Australia	$32,900
United Kingdom	$31,400
Mexico	$10,600
Pakistan	$2,600
Haiti	$1,800
Ethiopia	$1,000
Zambia	$1,000
Afghanistan	$800
Somalia	$600

> *Presidential visit*

U.S. President George W. Bush talks to patrol
commanders on a visit to the Mexico border in 2006.

Immigration – Is It Good Or Bad For A Country?

Many people support the call for restricting the number of immigrants who can enter a country. Some go even further, and argue that immigration should be stopped altogether. Why? They believe that immigration is a bad thing, and harms a nation's **economy**, culture, and society. Other people say there should be few restrictions. In their opinion, immigration is a good thing for a country. It boosts the economy, and brings variety and freshness.

This book will help you decide which viewpoint you support. But first you have to examine a vital question. Are all immigrants the same, and do they deserve the same treatment? It is important to understand that there are two kinds of immigrant—legal and illegal. Today, most national governments have strict controls regarding immigration. They allow only a fixed number of people to settle in their country. Other foreigners are permitted to enter the country for a temporary stay. These are the "legal" immigrants.

However, there are many thousands (maybe millions) more who are desperate to move to another country. They cannot get official permission to immigrate, but they travel anyway. These people enter a country in a variety of ways—hidden from official eyes. They are "illegal" immigrants. Should they be stopped? Can they be stopped?

Crossing the border: the United States and Mexico

The land border between Mexico and the United States stretches for 3,140 kilometres (1,950 miles). Much of it is harsh desert. About 350 million people cross this border every year—legally. But another million (mostly Mexicans) cross it illegally. The U.S. government puts a vast amount of money into guarding this border with soldiers, fences, **radar**, video systems, and "spy in the sky" aircraft.

Is it worth it? Do controls work? Ask yourself:

- Why do so many Mexicans risk their lives to reach the United States?
- What are the other dangers for illegal immigrants in the border area?
- Why should the U.S. government spend millions of dollars trying to stop them?
- Do you believe all the information given?

Look at this article and for other evidence to help you answer these questions.

President Bush's Plan to Stem Tide of Illegal Immigrants

Bush is seeking money from Congress for the deployment of up to 6,000 National Guard troops to help Border Patrol agents.

"They will operate **surveillance** systems, build **infrastructure**, analyze intelligence, and provide training," Bush said.

Bush said that since he took office in 2001 the number of border agents has increased from 9,000 to nearly 12,000. New fencing, lighting and cameras have been added in key locations.

"We're in the process of making the border the most technologically advanced in the world," Bush said. Opponents contend the barriers would shift illegal immigrant and smuggling traffic to areas of the border without fencing.

More than 85 percent of the illegal immigrants come from Mexico, and most are sent home within 24 hours.

[CNN Report 18th May 2006]

> *Caught in the act*

U.S. Border Patrol agents detain three illegal immigrants near the Mexican border at Fasabe, Arizona, in 2006. An astounding 1.1 million illegal immigrants were arrested along the U.S.—Mexico border in 2006.

Illegal immigration slang

Various slang terms have come into use for people smugglers and illegal immigration:

Coyote Someone paid to smuggle illegal immigrants across the Mexican border into the United States

Corridor of Death Part of the Sonoran Desert that runs from the Mexican state of Sonora into the U.S. state of Arizona. Hundreds of migrants die every year trying to cross into the United States by this route. They can fall prey to dangerous bandit gangs as well as the extreme heat and difficult terrain.

General Person who organizes immigrant groups and gets them into freight wagons

Snakehead Someone who smuggles people from China into the United States or Western Europe

For restricting illegal immigration

"The ongoing migration of persons to the United States in **violation** of our laws is a serious national problem **detrimental** to the interests of the United States."
Ronald Reagan, former U.S. President

"I'm deeply sympathetic to the huge numbers of people looking to come here today to escape suffering and poverty in their own lands. But as a country, we cannot afford to have a total open-door policy without any restrictions on entry."
Ed Koch, former Mayor of New York

"They'll flood our schools. Our health-care system will collapse, and our social service system will end up being overtaxed. We've got to get control of our borders, because if we don't, we're going to see our economy collapse."
James Sensenbrenner, U.S. House of Representatives

Are illegal immigrants bad for the United States?

There is no doubt that illegal immigration makes a big impact on the United States. Large numbers of foreign nationals enter the country and settle there every year. Does this non-stop flow of newcomers damage U.S. society? Many people think so. They say illegal or uncontrolled immigrants will

- Take jobs from native-born Americans. (There are only so many jobs to go round. If immigrants take them, it means more American nationals will be unemployed.)
- Accept lower wages than non-immigrants. (This means that wages will be lower for everybody.)
- Swamp the welfare system. (Huge numbers of poor immigrants claim welfare, education, and health benefits from the government. This means that American citizens have to pay higher taxes to finance the extra demand.)
- Change the country's national identity. (Foreigners bring their own habits and customs with them, including different languages, foods, clothes, and religious beliefs. These are bound to have an effect on American culture.)
- Increase the risk of terrorist attacks. (Religious **fundamentalists** and other extremists could enter the United States, and then plan deadly strikes.)

Looking at the evidence

Is this all true? What evidence can you find that would make you agree or disagree with these claims? Look for facts about employment and wage levels

> *Strong opinions*
Anti-illegal immigration protesters demonstrate on Capitol Hill, Washington, D.C., demanding tougher border controls and a crackdown on illegal immigrants.

throughout the nation, and for **statistics** about welfare claimants. Read about the lifestyles of some of the most recent legal immigrants to the United States, such as the Vietnamese and Afghan people from Asia. Think about national security.

Ask yourself: why do some people object so strongly to immigration? Obviously, many arguments can be backed up with facts and figures, particularly as regards illegal immigration. But is there something more?

All through history, people have been alarmed by foreigners. This feeling is called "xenophobia" (a Greek word meaning "fear of strangers"). Many people in the world today believe that their countries belong to people who were born there. In their view immigrants, legal or illegal, simply do not belong.

 ## Taking jobs from others?

The number of Mexican immigrants in the whole U.S. labour market is approximately 3.5 percent. The proportion of Mexican immigrants in the U.S. industrial workforce by occupation is as follows:

Agriculture and forestry	15.5 percent
Construction	8.5 percent
Manufacturing	7.0 percent
Mining	3.0 percent
Transport and warehousing	2.5 percent

(Figures taken from most recent U.S. census information)

Benefits of immigration

"Everywhere immigrants have enriched and strengthened the fabric of American life."
John F. Kennedy, former U.S. President

"Remember, remember always, that all of us ... are descended from immigrants and revolutionists."
Franklin D. Roosevelt, former U.S. President

"The high-tech world we are now dominating is dependent on educated folks, but we're short of workers. It is to our nation's advantage to encourage high-powered, smart people to come into our country."
George W. Bush, U.S. President

"Legal immigrants have long come to America seeking a fair chance to contribute and, in the process, have enriched our culture and strengthened the nation. Immigrants have always pulled their weight."
George Soros, financier and philanthropist

"It's thanks to us that this country is what it is to this day, and what it will be for the future."
Ardaya Barron, Bolivian immigrant

Is immigration good for the United States?

Most immigrants move to the United States to find a better quality of life. They look for the benefits of living in a wealthy, powerful and developed nation. But do immigrants bring benefits to U.S. life? Supporters of increased immigration say that legal newcomers:

- actually make the United States wealthier. (Economists reckon that immigrants add U.S. $20 billion a year to the economy—that is, about U.S. $80 for each U.S.-born resident.)
- allow many companies to profit from cheap labour costs. (This means that they can sell their goods cheaper, so consumers also profit.)
- enrich U.S. society by bringing in fresh cultural influences. (The United States is already a bewildering and exciting mixture of world cultures.)
- strengthen the workforce. (Immigrants tend to take the "dirtier" jobs, such as cleaning and fruit picking, which Americans are reluctant to do. Without immigrant labour, there would be employment shortages in these areas.)

> *New Americans*

A group of 250 legal immigrants take the oath of loyalty to the United States during a citizenship ceremony in Miami, Florida.

 ## New life in the new world

The Statue of Liberty in New York Harbor is a symbol of freedom and a new beginning. It was the first thing many immigrants saw as they neared the United States. In 1883 Emma Lazarus wrote a poem in which the statue speaks:

"Give me your tired, your poor,
Your huddled masses, yearning to breathe free,
The wretched refuse of your teeming shore.
Send these, the homeless, tempest-tost to me:
I lift my lamp beside the golden door."

A century later, have Americans changed their minds?

> *Searching for safety*

Over 300 migrants from Eritrea, East Africa, are crammed into this small boat. It was spotted by Italian coastguards in the Mediterranean Sea and brought to safety.

Should We Shelter People Who Are In Danger?

So far, this book has looked at the practical side of the debate about immigration. This can include the threat to jobs and welfare, the dangers of overcrowded housing in cities, and the effects of foreign cultures.

But the immigration argument also has a moral side. This includes questions about how we should behave towards other inhabitants of the world. Is it right or wrong to restrict the number of foreigners who can enter our country? Shouldn't we welcome people who are searching for safety and an escape from poverty and fear?

After all, those who live in the wealthy and developed nations of the world are very lucky. Most of them enjoy a high standard of living—enough to eat, good medical services, protection from violence. They also enjoy many kinds of freedom—freedom to elect their own leaders, to express their own opinions, and to follow their chosen religious faith.

For many people, however, the world is a harsh and frightening place. Poverty, war, **repression**, and natural disaster can make life unbearably hard. It is not surprising if large numbers want to give themselves a better chance by finding a new home elsewhere. This is exactly what migrants have done all through human history. Has anyone got the moral right to stop them? Should they not be given the chances your ancestors had?

The Tampa Case

On 26 August 2001, a fishing boat from Indonesia was drifting helplessly in the Indian Ocean. It was crammed with 438 refugees who had fled from Afghanistan. The Norwegian cargo ship *Tampa* came to their rescue and took them aboard.

The *Tampa*'s captain decided to take them back to Indonesia. But the refugees wanted to go to Australia. They said they would all jump overboard rather than go back. The captain agreed to drop them at Christmas Island, part of Australian territory.

But the story turned nasty. The Australian government did not want the refugees, and told the *Tampa* to keep out of its waters. Soldiers boarded the ship and found many of the refugees were badly sick. In the end, the Afghans were loaded onto another vessel and taken to **detention camps** on the Pacific island of Nauru.

What happened next

The incident caused a scandal in Australia and round the world. It highlighted the two sides of the immigration debate. Was the Australian government being selfish and avoiding its human rights duties? Or was it showing a strong and determined attitude towards illegal immigrants? There were supporters on both sides.

Over the following months the 438 Afghans from the *Tampa* were joined in the camps by hundreds of other illegal immigrants. They were part of a wave of Asian people who made the dangerous journey looking for "asylum", or refuge, in Australia. Some were eventually allowed to settle in New Zealand, while others were kept imprisoned on Nauru for several years.

Why keep them out? What Australian politicians said ...

✔ The asylum seekers were simply "queue-jumpers", falsely claiming to be refugees in order to gain illegal entry into the country—ahead of those who had applied in the proper way.

✔ If Australia accepted these boat people, the floodgates might open. "People smugglers" would see Australia as a soft target, and bring in many more illegal immigrants.

✔ The group of Afghans might contain terrorists in disguise.

> *Without a home*

Some of the rescued refugees camp out beneath the towering stacks of cargo containers on board the *Tampa* in the Indian Ocean in August 2001.

 ## Captain under pressure

The captain of the *Tampa* was Norwegian Arne Rinnan. He was put in a very difficult position. On the one hand his new refugee passengers were unwilling to be disembarked in Indonesia, to the point where they would rather lose their own lives. On the other hand, he had the Australian government saying his ship could not enter its waters. All he could do was sit tight and wait. Rinnan told a BBC reporter at the time: "If we move, they say they will go crazy, and threaten with jumping ship, so for the safety of everybody I stay put."

The Australian government was not happy with Rinnan's stance. It listened in to his phone conversations from the ship and eventually sent in its army to clear off the refugees on to Christmas Island. Others around the world saw his actions as wise and humane. He was knighted by the King of Norway for his bravery and humanitarian values. In the time since the *Tampa* crisis, Captain Rinnan has been named Shipmaster of the Year by the Nautical Institute and also by Lloyds List (the world's leading shipping information service). Commenting on his actions, the Norwegian Shipowners' Association said "To us it is self evident that people in distress are rescued regardless of who they are and where they come from."

Why did they leave their homeland?

Why did the Afghans set out in an overcrowded and leaky boat to cross a vast area of perilous ocean? They had paid a lot of money for the voyage, and put their lives in great danger. What drove them to do it?

The 438 travellers were refugees (people seeking a refuge from danger). They had left their homeland because they believed their lives were under threat. Their country, Afghanistan, had been ruled since the late 1990s by a hardline group called the **Taliban**. The Taliban persecuted anyone who disagreed with them, imprisoning, killing, and maiming their victims, and imposing harsh laws. Ordinary life became a nightmare for many Afghan people, and large numbers decided to emigrate.

> *Let them go!*

People who disagreed with the Australian government detaining refugees on Nauru protested on the streets of Sydney in 2005, halting rush-hour traffic.

How many refugees?

The United Nations High Commissioner for Refugees (UNHCR) is an agency of the United Nations Organization, which works for the welfare of refugees throughout the world. Here are some of the most recent UNHCR statistics (2004):

Refugees who are homeless, but still in their country of origin	8 million
Refugees in camps near the borders of their country of origin	10 million
Refugees who are seeking asylum overseas	1 million
Others	3 million
Total number of refugees worldwide	22 million

Should refugees get special treatment?

The 438 travellers rescued by the *Tampa* were refugees. But were they a special case? Did they deserve different treatment from other immigrants trying to become citizens in Australia? After all, most of the world's refugees do not go far. They stay in or close to their own country, hoping that one day they will be able to go home.

Were the *Tampa* refugees different from other illegal immigrants? They did not move across the world in search of better job prospects or better education or better housing. They left their homeland because they feared for their lives. Do you think the Australian government should have allowed them in immediately?

What are asylum seekers?

Asylum seekers are a special type of refugee. They travel to another country to claim "asylum"—a safe place where they will be protected from arrest or persecution by their own government. They have to apply for asylum status, and may have to show that they would be in danger of their lives if they were forced to return home.

Is it easy to be accepted for asylum? The process can take a very long time. Meanwhile, the asylum seekers often have to live in detention camps (like the *Tampa* refugees) for months or even years. This can be a distressing time. The conditions in the camps are sometimes appalling, with a lack of proper food, water, and medicines, and families being split up. Some refugees go on hunger strike in protest at their harsh treatment.

Downfall of a people smuggler

What sort of people take money to smuggle refugees illegally into another country? These people are certainly breaking the law. Here is the story of what happened to one of them when he was finally arrested and tried in court. There are many people smugglers all over the world who become wealthy through this trade in humans. Why do you think anyone would pay to become an illegal immigrant?

Jailed for 8½ years: ringleader of human traffickers who thought they were invincible

Thursday October 5, 2006

A ringleader of one of Europe's biggest people-smuggling rackets, which is thought to have brought thousands of illegal immigrants into the UK, was jailed yesterday for 8½ years.

Ramazan Zorlu, 43, played a key role in a huge network, which earned its organizers millions of pounds. Men, women, and children were smuggled on lengthy journeys across Europe, using planes, trains, lorries, and even light aircraft — often in appalling conditions, hidden in tiny secret compartments, sometimes going without food and water for days …

Detective Chief Superintendent Maxine De Brunner of Scotland Yard said it was the most significant human smuggling ring ever investigated and prosecuted in the UK. British police intercepted more than 400 illegal immigrants during the investigation, but believe that thousands more may have succeeded in evading detection. She said: "Human smuggling is an appalling crime. The criminal networks have no regard for the safely of those being smuggled. The smuggling of humans often involves them being transported for days or long periods of time without food or water in dangerous concealed compartments on the undercarriage of a lorry …

Judge Nicholas Ainley, sentencing Zorlu, said: "I find it hard to conceive of a more serious case of this type of offence coming before the courts." … "You must have been considering these people more as commodities than individuals to be cared for."

[Rosie Cowan, Crime Correspondent
The Guardian]

Questions to ask yourself:

- Should men like Ramazan Zorlu be seen as criminals? They claim they are helping immigrants on their quest to find a new and better life.
- Why do people have to hide in "secret compartments" and other horrible places? Many illegal immigrants have died of suffocation during their journeys.
- What sort of travel documents do refugees need before they are legally allowed to enter another country? What do you need when you visit abroad?
- How many "people-smugglers" or "human traffickers" are there around the world? They certainly operate in many countries, though nobody knows how many illegal immigrants they transport.
- Would there be fewer refugees in foreign countries if there were no people-smugglers? Crossing a border illegally would be much more difficult.
- Is there a difference between a "people-smuggler" and a "human trafficker"? See what evidence you can find.

Price of a new life

How much do illegal immigrants pay to be smuggled into another country? In 2005, the average price for one person to be transported from Asia into the United States or United Kingdom was estimated to be £30,500 (U.S.$60,000).

> *See-through smuggling*

This image was taken by an X-ray machine, and shows people hidden inside a lorry. Machines like this are used at French and British English Channel ports.

Who is to blame?

What makes refugees run away from the country where they were born? There are many answers, as this book has shown. Amongst the most important of them is fear. People flee from civil war, invasion, tyranny, and all other human-made disasters that create brutality and violence.

So, can we blame the people who start wars and rule by terror? Without these horrible things there would certainly be fewer asylum seekers and innocent displaced refugees. Afghanistan, for example, has suffered from two major invasions, a long and bitter civil war, and a repressive regime within the last 30 years. Millions of Afghans have emigrated. If the violence had not occurred, they would have stayed at home.

There are plenty of others who could be blamed for increasing the flood of refugees and other immigrants to the developed countries of the world. What about the people who make a profit from illegal immigrants? The smugglers have grown rich—and the more migrants they move, the more money they make. The "**gangmasters**" and other businesspeople who employ the foreigners have also become wealthy because they can pay very low wages. Their illegal workers are in no position to argue.

 Fleeing the bloodbath of war

The United Nations High Commissioner for Refugees (UNHCR) calculates that 12 percent of all Iraqis have fled their homes since the 2003 U.S.-led invasion. Where are most of them now?

Inside Iraq, but displaced	1.7 million
In Syria	1 million
In Jordan	700,000
In Egypt	80,000
In Lebanon	40,000
(Figures for January 2007)	

What happens to asylum seekers in the United Kingdom?

About 23,500 asylum seekers arrived in the United Kingdom in 2006 and applied for refugee status.

Asylum seekers are supposed to state immediately upon entering the country that they are coming in as asylum seekers and not under any other category, such as student or tourist. If it seems very likely (usually based on the country the asylum seeker has come from) that the application for asylum will be refused, the applicant will be sent to a designated "fast-track" centre for cases that are easy to decide.

All others go to induction centres where they are issued with identity cards that contain a picture, fingerprint, and details of age and nationality. These asylum seekers become part of the system and their cases get dealt with in due course. Those that are seen as likely to "disappear", and not make contact when advised to, are sent to detention centres until their cases come up. Every year a large number of asylum seekers fail to get permission to stay in the UK. In 2006, 16,250 were rejected and removed from the country.

In 2006, the five countries where most asylum seekers came from to the United Kingdom were Iran, Afghanistan, Eritrea, the Peoples' Republic of China, and Somalia.

A harsh deterrent

Why is the asylum procedure so complicated? Why is the detention policy so harsh? Speaking of asylum seekers arriving by sea, a spokesperson answered: "In order to deter others from taking the life-threatening boat trip and ensure our **maritime** defense assets are not diverted from their national security mission."
U.S. Immigration, Customs and Enforcement (ICE)

> *Stopped at the border*
Mothers and children who have entered the United States illegally wait in a detention centre in Nogales, Arizona, after being arrested by border guards. About 27,000 illegal immigrants are in U.S. detention centres every night.

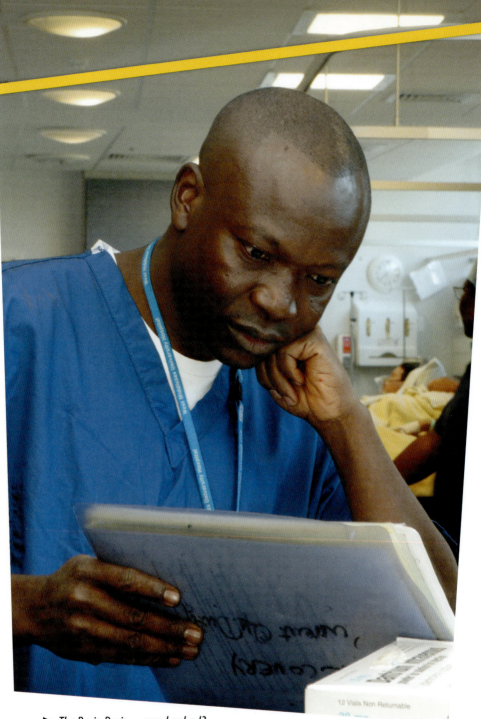

> *The Brain Drain—good or bad?*
Hospitals in developed countries are better equipped,
and pay and working conditions are better.

The Brain Drain

What is the most important issue in the immigration debate? Many people would say that it was the impact of immigrants on their new country, particularly illegal immigrants. Some call the impact damaging, while others call it beneficial. In any case, the focus of attention is usually on the destination of the migrants.

There is another side to the argument, which is often forgotten. What happens to the country that is left behind? What effect does the disappearance of part of the population have on the people that remain? In some cases, it might bring advantages – less overcrowding, and less competition for jobs and resources. Workers overseas often benefit their native countries by sending home regular sums of money.

However, there is also a crucial downside. A significant number of migrants come from the educated **professional** classes. Doctors, nurses, teachers, and engineers are attracted to other countries because they will get better pay, conditions, and opportunities. Few ever return to their homelands. This kind of emigration is called "the brain drain". The loss of intelligent, talented, and highly trained people is a serious blow to any country. Statistics show that it hits small and developing countries the hardest, because they can least afford to lose a valuable part of the workforce. Where do these brains end up? The majority migrate to wealthy, developed regions, such as the United States, Australia, and the European Union.

The Ever Grim Story of Brain Drain

A report from the World Health Organization (WHO) says that in Africa alone, where health needs and problems are greatest, around 23,000 qualified **academic** professionals emigrate annually to Europe and the Americas in search of better life opportunities.

Roughly 50 percent of the total population of doctors in Ghana are practising in the USA alone; while between 70 and 100 doctors emigrate from South Africa every year. Nigeria alone loses more health workers than other African countries combined. Some estimates put the number of Nigerians outside at one out of every ten black doctors in the U.S.

The migration is already causing havoc to the country and the growth of its health care system. There has been a reduction in the number of newly registered doctors from 1,750 in the year 2000 to 800 in 2002, a 60 percent reduction.

The migration is a major health disaster in most African nations. For instance, it is alarming and pathetic that Malawi, a small poor African country has more of its doctors practising in Manchester, England, than in all of Malawi.

According to the WHO report, a typical Nigerian health professional in the U.S. contributes about $150,000 per year to the U.S. economy.

[*The Guardian*, Thursday, 5 May 2005]

Who loses the most?

This WHO report concentrates on how the Brain Drain affects one continent—Africa. Do you find the quoted figures shocking? What are these nations losing besides their skilled professionals? Most of them have schools and colleges that give a good education. If the best qualified pupils emigrate, then that education, and the investment behind it, will be lost to another country.

Why are African countries so vulnerable? Look for evidence about the economic conditions in the places that are mentioned in the extract. You will see that most of them suffer from widespread poverty, which is partly caused by natural disasters such as drought and contagious disease. These can lead on to other social problems, including high crime rates and industries that fail due to lack of money.

The Brain Drain worldwide

Is Africa the worst hit? There are many other developing countries throughout the world—especially in Asia and Central and South America. Many doctors, teachers and other trained men and women leave these places too, seeking better opportunities in wealthier lands. Do they suffer as badly as Nigeria and Malawi?

The larger countries seem to feel the effects of the Brain Drain less severely. Nations such as India, Brazil, and China lose just as many professionals to emigration. But because they have big populations, the loss does not seem so great. Countries with small populations, such as Haiti or Jamaica, are much more badly harmed. Nearly 80 percent of people who get college degrees there end up working abroad.

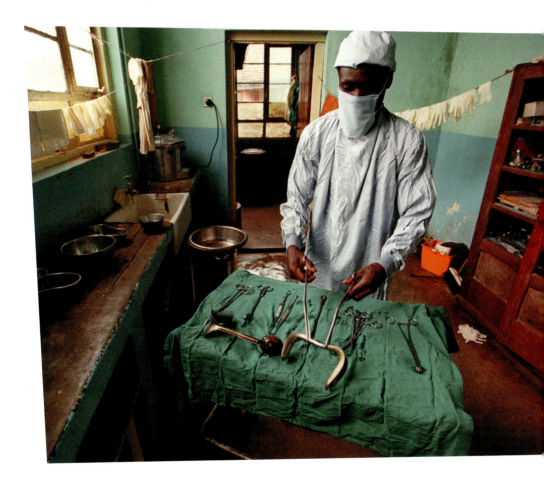

> *Difficult conditions*

This surgeon in Tanzania is preparing his operating room for a patient. The conditions in a modern, Western hospital would make his job much easier.

Why do so many professionals emigrate?

The direction of the Brain Drain is usually the same: from the poorer, developing countries to the rich countries. So the reasons why highly educated people want to move are much the same as other migrants. They are looking for better pay, better living conditions, and better opportunities to be successful. Many are also fleeing violence, corruption, or instability in their countries of origin.

But do some "brain drainers" have special reasons to go abroad? People who have gone through a long and hard period of training should be highly valued members of society. They expect to be well paid. They also expect to work in

> *Modern facilities*

Not all hospitals in Africa are under-staffed and under-resourced. This modern, well-equipped hospital in Namibia is where Angelina Jolie and Brad Pitt's daughter was born.

The Brain Drain: what do they think?

"I feel guilty when I visit hospitals in Zambia. I work at an English hospital with many qualified anaesthetists on the staff. In the whole of Zambia, there is only one! The medical schools train them, but they all leave when they are qualified." *Farzin, an anaesthetist in the United Kingdom*

"I did my undergraduate degree in India, but did further study in Scotland. I got a job in England after that so I can't see myself going back. There aren't opportunities for the kind of work I want to do." *Grace, a management consultant originally from India*

"My parents were keen that we get the best education possible in circumstances where we were safe from violence. It's what any parent would want for their children." *Elaine, a bank manager in the United States who left Zaire (now the Democratic Republic of the Congo) as a teenager with most of her family*

places (such as hospitals and science laboratories) that are properly equipped and up-to-date. If they cannot find these at home, they will not be able to work at their best—so they leave.

No drain—no gain

Who stands to gain most from the Brain Drain? Obviously, the new host countries benefit from the arrival of highly trained specialists like doctors and scientists. They bring vital skills and intelligence that every society needs. They also take away skills and intelligence from their homelands.

But is this always a major loss? Sometimes, the emigrants are replaced by new immigrants. For instance, in recent years large numbers of Canadian professionals have moved to work in the United States. This obviously leaves a vital gap in Canada's workforce. But the gap has been filled by skilled immigrants arriving in Canada from other countries. This process has been called the "Brain Exchange".

> *Passport control*

A U.S. customs and border protection officer checks the passport of a new arrival at Miami International Airport in Florida.

What Has To Change?

Most of this book has been about the issues involved with controlling immigration. It has examined questions on both sides of the debate, using stories and statistics from the recent past.

Have you reached an opinion yet? You may have decided that too much immigration is harmful to a country, and it should be curbed by tougher new laws. Or maybe you believe that immigration brings huge benefits, and should not be restricted at all. Perhaps the best answer lies somewhere in between. One thing is certain. Immigration is having an enormous effect on our world. It can change societies and cause huge upheavals in the economy.

Clearly, the flow of people from one country to another is almost impossible to stop. But what can we do to change the present chaos? Can we go on allowing legal immigrants (and even more illegal ones) to arrive in such vast numbers? If we decide to restrict immigration still further, what sorts of measures are needed? Will they work?

Whether you are for or against more restrictions on immigration, it is clear the present system is not working well. It is not successful in keeping out illegal immigrants, or even of keeping count of them. For legal arrivals, the entry process is often long and complicated. All this must be improved before the many problems over immigration can be solved.

Should there be stricter controls?

Would better controls make the whole business of immigration easier? Some people argue that stricter laws and tougher barriers will stop illegal immigrants from entering a country. Dry up the flow of unwanted foreigners and there will be more money and time to spare for welcoming legal newcomers. This will make the processing of applications much quicker and easier.

Where should these new controls be targeted? Many immigrants enter a country through airports and seaports, where they can be easily spotted and identified. But many more cross land borders that are unguarded, or land from boats on remote parts of the coast. These are the areas that are the most difficult to patrol.

What methods can be used?

Passports have been around for hundreds of years, and were the first way of restricting immigration. A passport is proof of a person's nationality, and allows them to leave and return to their own country.

Now technology is providing many new and more accurate ways of checking someone's identity. Electronic systems can record a fingerprint, the **retina** of an eye, and even the pattern of a voice – all of these things are different for each of us. Thanks to modern science, there are also dozens of new ways of keeping watch on land borders. Very accurate long-range cameras are mounted on tall towers, or carried in unmanned "**drone**" aircraft. Electronic **sensors** detect heat from bodies or vibrations in the ground. Steel fences can be topped with razor wire or electrified. How effective will these new methods be?

The barrier billions

Here are U.S. government estimates for a barrier to run along the 3,219-kilometre (2,000-mile) Mexico border from the Gulf of Mexico to the Pacific:

3-metre (10-feet) high wire fence topped with razor wire
£433 million ($851 million)

The same fence, electrified
£617 million ($1.2 billion)

3.6-metre (12-feet) high, 0.3-metre (2-feet) thick concrete wall
£1 billion ($2 billion)

Double steel and wire fence with 91-metre (100-yard) gap, lights, and sensors
£4 billion ($8 billion)

Border barriers: do they work?

Here is a 2007 story from the website of Minuteman, a border watch organization that campaigns for a barrier along the US-Mexico border.

Minuteman Fence Rising on Border Ranch

The Minuteman Civil Defense Corps has financed and coordinated the construction of a 0.9-mile-long, 13-foot-high steel mesh fence east of Naco, Arizona. So far, about a quarter mile is finished. Although the barrier covers only a tiny section of the 362 miles of international border in Arizona, the Minuteman organization insists the impact on illegal immigration will be more than just symbolic. It will "let the government know that it's not as difficult to secure the borders as they lead us to believe". The barrier is expected to cost about $650,000.

> Block them out!

Workers fix metal mesh to high steel beams in the Arizona desert. This mile-long fence on the border between Arizona and Mexico has been paid for by an American anti-illegal immigration group, to show what can be done to close the border.

Should migrants be free to go anywhere they want?

Some people say there should be no restrictions at all on immigration. Everyone should be free to live and work wherever they like. This is called "open immigration". There are many opponents of this view.

Campaigners have two main arguments in favour of open immigration. First, they believe that rich countries should welcome migrants from poor countries and let them enjoy higher living standards. Keeping them out is simply being selfish. The second argument is practical. They say that the world should be a free market place, and that people should be allowed to go where there are jobs. The result will be a more balanced economic system throughout the world.

What would happen if immigration was totally unrestricted?

Nobody really knows the answer to this question. No country in recent history has ever lifted all restrictions on the entry of foreigners. For many decades, the United States had an almost open policy on new settlers (although it was limited mainly to Europeans). This policy ended with the Immigration Act of 1924, which introduced much stricter laws.

However, a few countries have recently made immigration much easier for some people. In Europe, for example, the 27 states of the European Union (the EU) passed a law giving freedom of movement to people who live there. Citizens of the member countries are free to move to another member country. They can live, work and even vote there without restrictions. This freedom has led to a huge migration of workers from poorer countries (such as Poland and Bulgaria) to richer ones.

 The most open country?

Canada has the highest immigration rate in the world. It admits more immigrants per head of its population than any other country. Every year, about 250,000 immigrants settle in Canada – that is, one new arrival for every 12 people already living there. Canada also has 34 large ethnic groups (of more than 100,000 each), and many smaller ones.

Here is a 2006 article from "Open Immigration", a website run by *Capitalism* magazine in the United States. Do you agree with the writer's views?

Open immigration: the benefits are great. The right is unquestionable. So let them come.

Entry into the U.S. should be free for any foreigner, with the exception of criminals, would-be terrorists, and those carrying infectious diseases.

An end to immigration **quotas** is demanded by the principle of individual rights. Everyone has rights as an individual, not as a member of this or that nation. One has rights not by virtue of being American, but by virtue of being human. One doesn't have to be a resident of any particular country to have a moral entitlement to be secure from governmental coercion against one's life, liberty, and property.

In the words of the Declaration of Independence, government is instituted "to secure these rights" — to protect them against their violation by force or fraud.

A foreigner has rights just as much as an American. To be a foreigner is not to be a criminal.

[www.capmag.com]

> *Open borders*

There are many unmanned crossings on the long border between the United States and Canada.

> *School debate*

This school debate in the United States has teams of three on each side.

How to organize your own debate

How much should immigration be restricted? Have you formed your own opinion yet? You should now plan to explain your views to other people and persuade them that you are right. The best way to do this is to organize a debate with your classmates.

What kind of debate?

An organized debate is the best kind. If a crowd of students get together and start arguing, they will most likely end up with a shouting match. You won't learn anything from that. Your debate has to have two equal sides. It also has to have rules and a structure that everybody agrees to.

There are many debate formats to choose from. The simplest of all is a classroom debate, in which every student gets a chance to argue their opinion. However, a formal debate is a lot more rewarding, even if it is more complex to set up. In this, you start with a **motion** (a question or a statement) to argue about. A specially chosen panel of speakers (usually three people each in two teams) represents each side of the argument.

Who takes part?

The essential ingredient for a debate is opposing viewpoints. It is vital to present different views on the topic being discussed, so that the audience is likely to hear something that challenges or appeals to them. Make sure you've found people to present both positions. One side argues in favour of a topic (this is called the **proposition**). The other side argues against the case made by the first speaker (this is called the **opposition**).

How long will it last?

Set a time limit for the whole debate. If possible, keep the total running time to no more than an hour. You should also set time limits for each of the speakers (no longer than five minutes). This will leave roughly 30 minutes for questions from the audience, and for voting at the end.

Who's in charge?

Choose someone to be the **moderator** (referee). The moderator does not take part in the debate but directs it, introducing the topic and keeping control of the speakers. Nobody may speak unless the moderator permits. A good moderator should treat both sides equally.

What happens?

The moderator explains the motion and the topic for debate. Then the speakers on the panel take turns to read their prepared speeches. After this, the moderator asks the audience to put questions to the speakers. The debate ends with short closing statements from both sides, restating their opinions with strong supporting evidence. Then the audience votes, either for or against the motion. The moderator counts the votes and announces the winner.

Debater's checklist

Remember to:

✔ Research your subject thoroughly
✔ Collect plenty of facts and evidence
✔ Concentrate on the strongest points in your argument
✔ Speak clearly and loudly enough for the audience to hear
✔ Listen carefully to what other debaters say
✔ Allow time for other people to express their opinions
✔ Make notes of the weak points in your opponent's speech

Conclusion, for and against

Here is a quick survey of reasons why immigration takes place, and some of the main arguments for and against further restricting immigration.

Pushes and pulls

Humans have migrated across the world for millions of years. Almost every person in every land is descended from an immigrant. But what makes people want to move in the first place? There are two main factors – "push" and "pull". The "push" factors – such as war, poverty, disease and natural disaster - drive people out of their homelands. The "pull" factors – safety, more jobs opportunities, better pay and better education – attract them to other countries.

Pluses and minuses

Are immigrants good or bad for a country? Many people think they bring plenty of benefits to their new home. They may increase its wealth, take on jobs which others ignore, and improve businesses by lowering labour costs. On top of this, their culture may enrich and refresh society. Others believe immigrants may bring harm to a country. They may take jobs from native-born citizens, cause overcrowding and swamp health and education services. Their cultural differences may increase divisions in society.

Refugees and asylum seekers

Thousands of people migrate because they are in fear of their lives. They flee from bloody wars and from government persecution. Many refugees ask for asylum—a safe place where they will be protected from arrest or ill-treatment by their own government. Sometimes they pay "people-smugglers" to transport them illegally across state borders. Should more wealthy and peaceful states welcome these refugees?

Drains and gains

Immigration frequently causes harm to the country which is left behind. Large numbers of highly trained professionals, such as doctors, nurses and teachers, are migrating to wealthier states where they find better pay and career opportunities. This is a huge loss for their original homeland, which gave them their education. It is called the "brain drain". The destination countries enjoy a "brain gain". Can this problem be solved?

> *What do you think?*

This cartoon is called "Mixed Message". It was drawn by Nick Anderson of the Texas newspaper, the *Houston Chronicle*. The "mixed message" it portrays is the conflict between the U.S. government position of doing all it can to control illegal immigration, and the employers' stance of wanting plentiful and cheap labour.

What do you think now?

Did you have a definite opinion about immigration when you started this book? Or had you never really thought about the subject before? This book is not aimed at persuading you to take a view one way or another. Its object is to show you both sides of the debate, and give you tips on how to think critically, how to find and look at evidence, and how to put your case effectively. So, what do you think, how much should immigration be restricted?

Find Out More

Projects

Are you descended from immigrants? Dig back into the roots of your own family. Ask older relatives about their ancestors, look into local records, and consult books and websites on genealogy (see below).

Do you want to emigrate? Ask your family and schoolmates if they would ever think of moving to another country. What are their reasons? Where would they go?

Make a list of famous and successful people in your country—politicians, musicians, athletes, artists, scientists. Find out how many of them are first- or second-generation immigrants.

Books

About immigration in general

A Century of Immigration: 1820–1924, Christopher Collier and James Lincoln Collier (Benchmark, 2000)

American Immigration: A Student Companion, Roger Daniels (Oxford University Press, 2001)

The Changing Face of North America: Mexican Immigration, Leeanne Gelletly (Mason Crest, 2004)

Immigrants: Your Country Needs Them, Philippe Legrain (Little Brown, 2007)

Sources of evidence

Illegal Immigration: Examining Issues through Political Cartoons, Ed. William Dudley (Tandem Library, 2003)

Immigration: Great Speeches in History, Ed. Michelle E. Houle (Greenhaven, 2004)

Refugees

Notes from My Travels: *Visits with Refugees in Africa, Cambodia, Pakistan and Ecuador*, Angelina Jolie (Simon & Schuster, 2003)

Human Cargo: A Journey Among Refugees, Caroline Moorehead (Vintage, 2006)

Refugee: It Happened to Me, Angela Neustatter (Franklin Watts, 2005)

Websites

Finding out about your ethnic background

www.pbs.org/wnet/aalives
Site of the film *African American Lives* (2006), which tells migrants' stories

www.rootsforreal.com
Full of information and tips about tracing your ancestors

All sides of the debate

www.migrationwatchuk.org
A group campaigning for much stricter controls on immigration.

www.openimmigration.com
Campaigning for free access for immigrants

Glossary

academic from a higher school or university level

bias in favour of one particular view or argument

detention camp place where refugees and other immigrants are held before they are allowed to live freely in a country

detrimental causing damage or harm to something

DNA (short for deoxyribonucleic acid) chemical in all living things that passes on information about an individual's genetic make-up

drone pilotless aircraft that is remotely controlled

economy managing of money and other resources of a country, community, or business

emigrant person who leaves their homeland and moves abroad

fundamentalist someone who believes very strongly that the basic principles of their religious faith are literally true and unchangeable

gangmaster person who employs a "gang" of illegal immigrants, who often work for little pay in harsh conditions

genetic relating to inherited traits and characteristics in humans

immigrant person who enters a foreign country, having left their own

Industrial Revolution name given to the period since about 1700, during which the development of new machines and production methods has caused enormous changes throughout the world

infrastructure basic facilities and systems (such as roads, railways, and water supplies) that a country needs to run smoothly

maritime near the sea, or concerned with ships and the sea

migrant person who moves from one region or country to another

moderator person who presides over a meeting or assembly; also known as a referee

motion	formal proposal or statement that forms the basis of a debate
opposition	case put by a speaker who is against (or disagrees with) a motion
oppression	using violence or unjust methods to persecute someone or keep them under one's control
persecution	ill-treating someone, or punishing them for their political or religious beliefs
professional	belonging to an occupation that requires a long training period and special qualifications (such as a lawyer, a doctor, or a teacher)
proposition	case put by a speaker who is in favour of (or agrees with) a motion
quota	stated number of foreign people that will be accepted by a country
radar	method of detecting objects by measuring how they reflect radio waves
repression	keeping people firmly, even cruelly, under control
retina	delicate layer that lines the inner part of the eye and sends messages to the brain
sensor	device (often electronic) that detects sound or movement
Soviet Union	also called USSR. This was a communist empire centred on Russia that lasted from 1922 to 1991
statistics	the collecting, organizing, and interpreting of figures and other information
surveillance	close observation of a person or group who are under suspicion
Taliban	Islamic fundamentalist movement that ruled Afghanistan from 1996 to 2001
violation	breaking of a law, or the injuring of people or property
workforce	all the workers who are available in one country or project

Index